THE BOOK OF PASTA

THE

BOOK

OF

PASTA

LEGEND

   🥣   Preparation time

   🍲   Cooking time

   ⑤   Five ingredients or fewer

   Ⓥ   Vegan

   🍴   Vegetarian

   🚫   Nut-free

   🥛   Dairy-free

TWO THOUSAND YEARS OF BEAUTY

Close your eyes and imagine. A room with a long table running down the center, set with the "nice" tablecloth for an important occasion: a lunch at home with the family. Generations in conversation, old friends chatting, clinking glasses. Suddenly silence falls. A large pan full of steaming pasta is carried into the room from the kitchen. With a confident gesture and a smile of pride, it is placed in the middle of the table. The guests look on with appreciation, meeting each other's gaze with complicity and the anticipation of what is being proffered. Smiles spread. May the party begin.

PASTA, AN ICON OF HISTORY AND CULTURE

Joy, home, family, friendship, passion, everyday life, celebration, flavor. This is what pasta represents for Italians, and this book was created with the intent of sharing just how much pasta is a part of their lives, and even their very DNA. Pasta is a product that has won universal adoration, but it is also a geographical, social, and cultural atlas that helps us to understand the great changes that occurred in agriculture and nutrition in the Mediterranean basin over the past two thousand years.

The story originates with the cultivation of durum wheat and the first farmers to discover one of the most useful plants in the world. It's a plant that feeds on sun and water, whose prodigious grains, if kept dry and sheltered following the summer harvest, last a long time, and which, when ground, become flour. After centuries of differing uses, human genius forged the modern idea of pasta, a combination of the best semolina—a coarse flour made from durum wheat—with water, then dried in the heat of the sun so as to preserve it.

Pasta began to spread throughout the countries bordering the Mediterranean thanks to a series of fortuitous agricultural, cultural, and industrial coincidences, changes, and social customs. Historian Massimo Montanari explains that pasta drying—initially a Middle Eastern custom—arrived in Italy following the Muslim conquest of Sicily; in 1152, geographer Muhammad al-Idrisi testified that in Trabia, near Palermo, "they produced an abundance of pasta which is exported a lot, to Calabria and other countries, both Muslim and Christian, in large shiploads." Dried, stored, and easily transportable, pasta was consumed by traveling sailors and sold in the markets of port cities such as Genoa, Bari, and Naples. As its popularity spread, so were the first tools created and the first professions linked to it born, with artisans becoming pasta makers. The first shapes were cut with blades (knives), while some technologies used in other fields were adapted for pasta production. This is the origin story of that small medieval bronze object called a die, a perforated matrix through which a soft mixture of durum wheat semolina and water is passed; it was first referenced by Cristoforo da Messisbugo, a cook at the court of Ferrara in the first half of the sixteenth century, and perfected by Neapolitan pasta makers over the next two centuries.

From as early as the beginning of the nineteenth century, there were 148 artisanal pasta factories in Liguria alone—a region in Northern Italy overlooking the sea, with the ideal climate for drying pasta. There was the same proliferation in other areas of Central and Southern Italy, such as Campania, Lazio, Sardinia, Sicily, and Abruzzo, regions with dry and well-ventilated coasts. Barilla's own history in Parma, an industrial city in Northern Italy located along the Via Emilia, is rooted in this fervor of the nineteenth century. Since the sixteenth century, the Barilla family were bread makers, also known as the "White Art" due to the color of the flours. In 1877, Pietro Barilla Sr opened a bread and pasta shop in Parma, passing the baton in 1910 to his sons Gualtiero and Riccardo, who would embrace the industrial era, constructing the very first factory. Since then, the growth of the Barilla brand has been closely intertwined with Italian food culture, making pasta a product accessible to all. The company would go on to establish itself as a world leader in the production of pasta, following a tradition of carefully selected ingredients, continuous research, constant technological innovation, and the meticulous study of shapes and recipes, always with a view to continuous improvement. Now in the twenty-first century, with Guido, Luca, and Paolo, the Barilla brand—still in the hands of the family that founded the company—has become synonymous with Italian quality throughout the world.

Pasta is a colorful and polyphonic novel, which is rewritten everyday by millions of people who interpret it, reread it, renew it. By people who love it, who appreciate its taste, but also its beneficial effect on the mind and spirit. The simplicity of the ingredients, a mixture of water and durum wheat semolina, should not mislead you, however; though basic in its composition, the production of pasta is not a trivial matter, and is full of nuance. Pasta makers, chefs, and designers have poured their imagination and creativity into pasta. And in this coming together of people, experiences, nature, and simplicity, isn't pasta a way of reshaping and enjoying the world?

RECIPES… AND MORE

This is not just a book of tasty recipes. These pages also tell lesser-known stories: those of the people who made pasta great, the mistakes from which strokes of culinary genius were born, passing through those ingredients that enhance the flavors of pasta. It evokes images and experiences that are both ancient and modern at the same time—of the aromas through windows opening onto the sea, of small artisan shops, of fishermen pulling their nets, of incomprehensible dialects (which somehow make sense), of hills swaying with ears of corn, of steam flowing out of a saucepan, the unmistakable scent of good-ness floating in whispers to your nose. Pasta is an everyday element that has conquered the kitchens of the world, becoming a way of life, uniting Alfredo alla Scrofa of Rome with the early twentieth-century Spaghetti Houses of New York, and linking the Via Veneto of Fellini's *Dolce Vita* with the best London restaurants between South Kensington and Belgravia. You can find a bit of Italy everywhere.

And so, all the recipes in this volume have been designed and developed to enhance the peculiarities of the various pasta shapes and styles by chefs from the Academia Barilla.

A meeting place between culture and food, between tradition and experimentation, the Academia was founded in 2004 in Parma, a UNESCO city of gastronomy.

In the Everyday Gatherings chapter, you will find deliciously simple recipes that are perfect to share with family and friends, created from the wide variety of shapes offered by the Barilla Classic range—testimonies of a unique heritage. The journey of pasta continues in Gourmet Meals, with a nod to food enthusiasts and all those who seek novelty and love to experiment with new combinations. Here you will find the rough and full-bodied surfaces of Barilla bronze-drawn pastas that provide vibrant gastronomic experiences. In Embracing Creativity you will discover the special shapes created by Barilla, as well as authentic regional pasta shapes—spokespersons of knowledge, style, and territory, which are today reimagined in a variety of new and creative recipes. Living Well offers recipes dedicated to new and healthy lifestyles, where naturalness and well-being are more central than ever. Whole grain (wholemeal), gluten free, and legume pasta, born from Barilla's experience and commitment to good food, become the protagonists of dishes cooked in the name of sustainability. Finally, how can we not talk about the most iconic pasta? Spaghetti is an Icon is an homage to the famous shape, n. 5, a cult all of its own, and thanks to which the Barilla brand is today a world ambassador of this extraordinary emblem of taste.

Pasta is a joy for the palate, but it can also satiate the spirit. Pasta is goodness and authenticity. And when a plate of spaghetti or rigatoni with tomato sauce is placed in front of you, you gather around the table willingly, happy to savor it and share a gesture of love. The time has come to boil the water with a generous amount of salt, choose your favorite shape from the pantry, cook it, drain it, and season it. Let the show begin.

EVERYDAY GATHERINGS

SIMPLICITY IN SHARING

Is talking about pasta the same as talking about love? Far be it from us to compare ourselves with such inspired authors as Petrarca, Gaspara Stampa, William Shakespeare, and Emily Dickinson; the love that we would like to talk about is that for pasta, a love common to all Italians, and which finds its greatest expression in company. It is while cooking and eating pasta that families unite, that faraway friends come together once more. Pasta builds bridges and brings joyful moments to life. Here, you will read about the love of those who have been able to give life to pasta, making it accessible and appreciated all over the world.

In its composition, pasta is indeed simple, but it took centuries of genius and experimentation to make it into the unique ingredient we know today. The invention of flours, the considered blending of them with water, and then the skilful process-ing—all led to a dough that has never gone out of fashion, but instead has been enriched with an extraordinary range of shapes, meanings, and uses. This is where Italian pasta makers come onto the scene: pioneers, innovators, experimenters, and conservatives, but also popularizers. Credit must also be given to the entrepreneurs who understood the potential of this product and decided to invest in it, and to the chefs who through time and among the steam of the kitchens created thousands of interpretations of pasta, which have conquered all kinds of palates in all kinds of places.

It's not just a matter of warming the soul, which could also be said of many other ingredients. A well-cooked plate of pasta is a pleasure that involves all the senses: while it is still cooking, its unmistakable starch scent reaches the nose, a comforting promise of a harmonious bond with the sauce, which in turn heralds revealing, persuasive aromas. The eyes enjoy every phase of the preparation: lingering briefly on the colors of the sauce, then on the proportions of the chosen pasta shape in comparison to the composition and texture of the sauce, and projecting the final result to the mind. The mouth is watering. Consistency and body are first tested by the fork's hold on the pasta shape, but full appreciation comes only with the first bite, when the tastebuds can truly enjoy the magic of the union. Then comes a gratification that reverberates with energy, positivity, well-being, and joy. And the effect is contagious—in an instant, the taste of a good pasta dish in company amplifies the beauty of sharing moments with others.

So in Italy, when lunchtime strikes, you can bet that at least one Italian out of two is sitting at a table in front of a steaming portion of pasta—short or long—a fork in hand ready for the most compelling dilemma: pierce one piece at a time, or group them together? Because pasta should not simply be eaten, much less while standing or walking. It must be enjoyed, and to make the most of it, the Italians set the table, make themselves comfortable, taking their time—perhaps fixing a large white napkin behind their neck to freely splash themselves with sauce, à la Jackson Pollock, without any fear of getting dirty, and above all without interrupting the pleasure of the tastebuds. Palate and spirit benefit equally.

But the beauty of pasta also lies in its ability to marry with all kinds of ingredients. Its most trusted interlocutors include the tomato, with which it shares a winning combination that, along with extra virgin olive oil—the cornerstone of the Mediterranean diet codified by Ancel Keys (page 270)—and cheeses such as Parmigiano Reggiano, mark in the collective imagination a sort of archetype of Italian taste. But there are also many other classic "dressings" that pasta loves to wear: from Ragù to Pesto alla Trapanese, from Gricia to Amatriciana, from Carbonara to Norma. All are authentic symbols of Italian cuisine, which many Italian immigrants across the world missed to the extent of revisiting them with whatever was available to them, effectively creating new recipes that brought back the flavor and joy of home.

Happiness truly lies in the little things: every Italian, as a child, spent time in the kitchen with their nonna, preparing the local pasta and secretly stealing a tagliatella here, a trofia there, an orecchietta or a raviolo left unattended on the cutting board, always raw. After all, cooking in Italy is ultimately a product of tradition, where you learn what is not taught in schools. Preparing a dish of pasta is a pleasure and a joy, and therefore every detail counts, from the choice or availability of a certain shape, to the selection of ingredients in order to create the most suitable seasoning. But it is also a set of ritual gestures, complicit glances, expert tastings, and emotions that filter between generations in the kitchen, where grandmothers summon their grandchildren and the latter observe and learn, and perhaps, smartphone in hand, create a video to immortalize the care and attention.

Pasta is a show that takes place every day in the kitchens of millions of homes, restaurants, and school canteens. Versatile, authentic, inclusive, it speaks a simple yet universal language; it raises discussions, but it also reconciles, and is above all democratic. Everyone can interpret it as they prefer. And tasting it will be a pleasure that, in company, only gets better.

The recipes you will find in this chapter are characterized by their refined simplicity—perfect to share with friends or to pull together in the evening after a day of work, and featuring a variety of Barilla Classic formats—penne, casarecce, farfalle, linguine, mezze maniche, tortiglioni, pipe, fusilli, conchiglie, rigatoni. Italians take care of themselves and their loved ones through food, and this comes most naturally to them through pasta.

CASARECCE WITH OLIVES, CAPERS, AND DATTERINO TOMATOES

25 min   20 min

SERVES 4

11 oz/320 g casarecce or mezze
  maniche
6 tablespoons extra virgin olive oil
1 shallot, finely chopped
1 tablespoon plus 1½ teaspoons
  capers, drained and rinsed
⅔ cup (3 oz/85 g) pitted Kalamata
  olives
5⅓ cups (28¼ oz/800 g) Datterino
  tomatoes, halved
oregano leaves, ripped into pieces,
  to serve
salt and freshly ground black
  pepper

Heat the oil in a medium pan over medium-high heat and sauté the shallot for 5 minutes until golden.

Add the capers and olives, mix well to combine, and cook for a further 2 minutes. Stir in the tomatoes and cook for 10 minutes. Season to taste.

In the meantime, cook the pasta in plenty of salted, boiling water according to the packet instructions. Drain when al dente and add to the sauce. Stir for a further 1 minute.

Before serving, sprinkle over the oregano leaves.

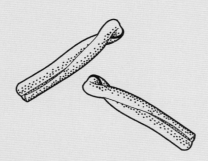

CASARECCE WITH CIME DI RAPA AND RICOTTA SALATA

15 min   12 min

SERVES 4

11 oz/320 g casarecce or gemelli
4 tablespoons extra virgin olive oil
1 clove garlic, sliced
1 dried chili pepper, chopped
2 anchovy fillets in oil
10½ oz/300 g cime di rapa
    (broccoli rabe), washed and any
    woody stalks removed
⅛ cup (1 oz/30 g) ricotta salata,
    grated
salt and freshly ground black
    pepper

Heat 3 tablespoons of oil in a wide, shallow pan over medium heat and fry the garlic, chili pepper, and anchovy fillets for 2 minutes, then add 4 tablespoons of water. Continue cooking for 5 minutes until the anchovies have broken up, then remove the pan from the heat.

In the meantime, cook the pasta in plenty of salted, boiling water according to the packet instructions, then add the cime di rapa with 5 minutes left of the cooking time.

A couple of minutes before draining the casarecce, reheat the fried garlic, chili pepper, and anchovies.

Drain the pasta when al dente, using a fine-meshed sieve to keep all the cime di rapa, then stir into the pan of garlic, chili, and anchovies.

Add the remaining oil, season with a grinding of fresh pepper, sprinkle with the ricotta, and serve immediately.

THREE-CHEESE FUSILLI
WITH PINK PEPPERCORNS

15 min   10 min

SERVES 4

11 oz/320 g fusilli or mini fusilli
5¼ oz/150 g Gorgonzola, cut into
   pieces
2½ oz/70 g Parmigiano Reggiano,
   grated
7 oz/200 g robiola, cut into pieces
1 cup (8 fl oz/250 ml) milk
handful of chives, finely chopped
salt and crushed pink peppercorns

Put the Gorgonzola, Parmigiano, and robiola in a pan with the milk over low heat, and leave to melt until creamy, about 3 minutes, stirring occasionally.

In the meantime, cook the pasta in plenty of salted, boiling water according to the packet instructions. Drain when al dente, reserving a cup of the pasta water, and tip the pasta into the pan of cheese. Mix over the heat for a couple of minutes until the melted cheese is perfectly blended with the pasta. If the sauce is too thick, add an extra spoonful of the pasta cooking water.

Serve with a sprinkling of finely chopped chives and crushed pink peppercorns.

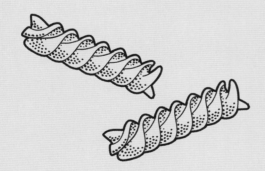

FUSILLI WITH RED RADICCHIO AND PARMIGIANO RINDS

Red radicchio shares the typically bitter taste of its chicory relative. Its union with Parmigiano Reggiano brings flavor and texture, giving birth to a dish that exudes the aromas of rural Veneto.

30 min   10 min

SERVES 4

11 oz/320 g fusilli or gemelli
5 tablespoons extra virgin olive oil
1 clove garlic, peeled and whole
14 oz/400 g red radicchio,
    julienned
⅔ cup (5¾ oz/160 g) ricotta
7 oz/200 g Parmigiano Reggiano
    rinds, scraped and diced
handful of chopped walnuts
salt and freshly ground black
    pepper

Heat 3 tablespoons of oil in a nonstick pan, add the garlic clove and fry for a couple of minutes, then add the radicchio and cook for 3 minutes. Add the ricotta, stir until completely melted, then add a pinch of salt and remove the garlic clove. Remove from the heat and set aside.

Cook the pasta in plenty of salted, boiling water according to the packet instructions, adding the diced Parmigiano rinds with the pasta so they become soft and stringy.

Drain the pasta when al dente and pour into a serving bowl with a drizzle of the remaining oil. Stir with a wooden spoon so it doesn't stick. Garnish with the radicchio sauce, stirring well, and sprinkle with the chopped walnuts and black pepper.

Tip
Parmigiano Reggiano rinds have a variety of uses in cooking: they can be added to a meat broth or a vegetable soup to give flavor, or cut into small pieces and put in the microwave for a few seconds to create crunchy chips. Before using, clean the exterior carefully to eliminate any impurities found on the surface.

MINI FUSILLI
WITH RED PESTO

Summer—a time of tomatoes slowly drying in the sun, and expert hands placing them in glass jars filled with extra virgin olive oil. They're great as a starter or as a filling for focaccia, and perfect for a pesto to garnish mini fusilli.

20 min   10 min

SERVES 4

11 oz/320 g mini fusilli or
   conchiglie rigate
4 tablespoons extra virgin olive oil
5¼ oz/150 g sun-dried tomatoes
   in oil, drained and coarsely
   chopped
1 clove garlic, peeled and whole
⅓ cup (1½ oz/45 g) pine nuts
1½ oz/45 g Parmigiano Reggiano,
   grated
salt and freshly ground black
   pepper

Heat 2 tablespoons of oil in a pan over medium-low heat and cook the tomatoes, garlic clove, and pine nuts, stirring often with a wooden spoon, until the pine nuts start to brown, 3–4 minutes.

Remove from the heat and pour the ingredients from the pan into a blender. Blend until creamy, then add a grinding of pepper and slowly pour in the remaining oil as you continue blending until you have a liquid sauce.

Transfer to a bowl and gradually add the grated cheese to thicken, stirring gently by hand with a wooden spoon.

In the meantime, cook the pasta in plenty of salted, boiling water according to the packet instructions.

Drain the pasta when al dente, coat with the sauce, and serve.

Tip
For a touch of freshness, garnish the dish with white celery leaves.

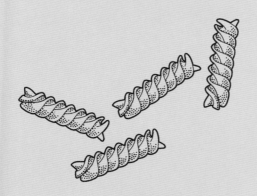

FUSILLI WITH EGGPLANT, TOMATOES, AND CAPERS

20 min   25 min

SERVES 4

11 oz/320 g fusilli or penne rigate
5 tablespoons extra virgin olive oil
1 onion, peeled and diced
2 eggplants (aubergines),
   cut into thin strips
7 oz/200 g cherry tomatoes,
   cut into wedges
1 dried chili pepper
¼ cup (1½ oz/40 g) capers, rinsed
basil leaves, to garnish
salt

Heat the oil in a pan over medium heat and sauté the onion for 5 minutes, followed by the eggplant (aubergine) for a further 5 minutes. Add the cherry tomatoes, chili pepper, and capers, and cook for around 15 minutes.

In the meantime, cook the pasta in plenty of salted, boiling water according to the packet instructions, and drain when al dente.

Toss the pasta in the sauce on the heat for a couple of minutes, then serve garnished with a few basil leaves.

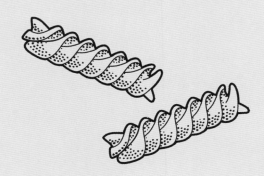

FUSILLI WITH VEGETABLE RAGÙ AND MOZZARELLA

40 min   15 min

SERVES 4

11 oz/320 g fusilli or mezze
    maniche
3½ oz/100 g eggplant (aubergine),
    diced
4 tablespoons extra virgin olive oil
1¾ oz/50 g leeks, thinly sliced
    (the white part)
1¾ oz/50 g celery stalk,
    diced
3½ oz/100 g carrot, diced
5¼ oz/150 g zucchini (courgettes),
    diced
5¼ oz/150 g red bell pepper, diced
5¼ oz/150 g yellow bell pepper,
    diced
1¼ oz/35 g shallot, diced
2 vine tomatoes, peeled,
    deseeded, and diced (see Tip)
basil leaves, coarsely chopped
1¾ oz/50 g mozzarella
salt

Place the eggplant (aubergine) in a colander, sprinkle with salt, and leave for around 30 minutes until they discard all their liquids.

Heat the oil in a pan over medium heat and brown the leeks together with the celery and carrot for 5 minutes. Then add the bell peppers, shallot, and eggplant, and cook for another 5 minutes.

Add salt to taste, then add the tomatoes and continue cooking for a few more minutes. Stir through most of the basil leaves.

In the meantime, cook the pasta in plenty of salted, boiling water according to the packet instructions. Drain when al dente, and stir through the vegetable ragù. Before serving, dot with the mozzarella and add a sprinkling of basil.

Tip
To peel and deseed a tomato, cut a cross in the base of the tomato, then place in a pan of simmering water for 15 seconds until the skin starts to pull away from the flesh. Transfer to an ice bath. Once cool, peel away the skin. Cut the tomato in half crosswise and scoop out the seeds with a spoon.

MOZZARELLA

The origin of the word "mozzarella" is linked to the production process of this famous cheese. The term comes from the Italian verb *mozzare*, which means "to break or cut." This refers to the characteristic gesture performed during processing: once the milk has been heated and the rennet added to coagulate the casein, the resulting curd is then manipulated and molded, rolled into a ball, and broken or cut off.

The two most popular mozzarella are undoubtedly Bufala Campana PDO (Protected Designation of Origin) and Fiordilatte. The first is produced exclusively using buffalo milk and is typical of the regions of Central and Southern Italy, in particular Campania, Lazio, and Puglia: the PDO certifies both the geographical origin and the quality of the product. It stands out for its richer, more intense flavor and creamier consis-tency. Fiordilatte mozzarella is produced using cow's milk in several Italian regions. It has a more delicate flavor and a less creamy texture, and is appreciated for its freshness and versatility in the kitchen.

Fiordilatte mozzarella and Mozzarella di Bufala Campana are excellent table cheeses, often served as an appetizer or accompanied with fresh vegetables or cold cuts. A vital component in pizza, and often combined with basil and tomato, mozzarella is an ingredient in many pasta-based recipes, to which it lends an unmistakably fresh, Mediterranean flavor.

MEZZE PENNE WITH MARINATED TOMATOES AND RICOTTA SALATA

2 h 10 min   8 min

SERVES 4

11 oz/320 g mezze penne or fusilli

17½ oz/500 g ribbed tomatoes, deseeded and cut into thin strips

3 tablespoons plus 1½ teaspoons extra virgin olive oil

10 basil leaves

1 clove garlic, peeled and very finely chopped

¼ cup (2 oz/60 g) ricotta salata, grated

salt and freshly ground black pepper

Put the tomatoes in a large bowl with the oil, 8 basil leaves, garlic clove, salt, and pepper. Stir, and leave to marinate for 2 hours.

Cook the pasta in plenty of salted, boiling water according to the packet instructions. Drain when al dente and tip into the bowl of tomatoes.

Mix well and sprinkle with the grated ricotta salata and remaining basil leaves before serving.

MINI PENNE WITH ARUGULA PESTO

Ovid described arugula (rocket) as a "luxurious herb," not only good on the palate, but also an aphrodisiac. Excellent for health and wellbeing, and versatile in the kitchen, it lends this dish a decisive flavor.

25 min   10 min

SERVES 4

11 oz/320 g mini penne or fusilli
3½ oz/100 g arugula (rocket), washed and dried
generous ¾ cup (7 fl oz/200 ml) extra virgin olive oil
¼ clove garlic
generous ⅛ cup (¼ oz/10 g) pine nuts
¾ oz/20 g Parmigiano Reggiano, grated
salt

Place the arugula (rocket) in a blender with three-quarters of the oil, a pinch of salt, the garlic, and pine nuts and blend. Add the grated cheese and stir briefly to blend. Cover the pesto with a little of the remaining oil while you cook the pasta.

Cook the pasta in plenty of salted, boiling water according to the packet instructions. Drain when al dente, retaining a cupful of the cooking water, and put the pasta in a mixing bowl with the pesto. Add a little cooking water and a drizzle of oil to dilute and stir together.

Tip
To sweeten the intense flavor of the arugula (rocket), you can substitute half of it with baby spinach or fresh basil.

FARFALLE WITH FAVA BEANS AND FRIED BREAD

Fava (broad) beans are an ancient legume, a sacred food in many old civilizations. Together with leftover stale bread and a fun butterfly pasta shape, they create an elegant, authentic dish with a rustic feel.

20 min 15 min

SERVES 4

10½ oz/300 g farfalle or fusilli

3 tablespoons plus 1½ teaspoons extra virgin olive oil

3½ oz/100 g onion, chopped

17¾ oz/500 g fava (broad) beans (fresh or frozen), blanched and peeled

3½ oz/100 g day-old bread

salt

Heat one-third of the oil in a pan over medium heat and cook the onion for 5 minutes until browned. Add the fava (broad) beans and fry for a few minutes, then cover with 1 cup (8 fl oz/250 ml) water. Add salt and leave to cook for around 10 minutes, then use an immersion blender to blend to a thick cream.

Crumble the interior of the bread (no crusts) into a pan with the remaining oil and cook for 2–3 minutes until golden brown and crunchy.

In the meantime, cook the pasta in plenty of salted, boiling water. Drain when al dente and mix with the cream. Sprinkle with the fried bread to serve.

Tip
If you don't like fried foods, you can substitute the bread with lightly toasted pistachios to retain a crunchy note.

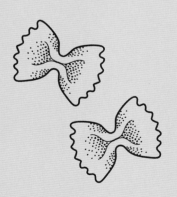

CONCHIGLIE RIGATE ALLA CRUDAIOLA

1 h 10 min   10 min

SERVES 4

11 oz/320 g conchiglie rigate
    or fusilli
14 oz/400 g tomatoes, deseeded
    and cut into thin strips
⅓ cup/80 ml extra virgin olive oil
8 basil leaves
1 clove garlic, chopped
4¼ oz/120 g cacioricotta cheese,
    grated
salt and freshly ground black
    pepper

Put the tomatoes in a mixing bowl with the oil, basil, garlic, salt, and pepper. Leave to marinate in the fridge for 1 hour.

Cook the pasta in plenty of lightly salted, boiling water according to the packet instructions. Drain when al dente and toss through the marinated tomatoes. Serve with a sprinkling of grated cacioricotta.

Tip
Leaving ingredients to rest for about 1 hour before using is an excellent way to add more flavor to any kind of sauce.

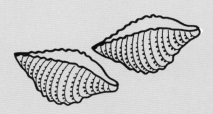

CONCHIGLIE RIGATE WITH CHERRY TOMATO CONFIT AND AROMATIC HERBS

15 min   1 hour

SERVES 4

11 oz/320 g conchiglie rigate
    or penne rigate
14 oz/400 g cherry tomatoes,
    halved
1 teaspoon confectioners' (icing)
    sugar
2¾ tablespoons extra virgin olive
    oil
1 clove garlic
1 sprig thyme
generous ¾ cup (7 fl oz/200 ml)
    milk
⅔ cup (5¼ oz/150 g) ricotta
2 tablespoons grated Pecorino
    Romano
handful of mixed fresh herbs
    (such as parsley, chervil,
    tarragon, chives), coarsely
    chopped
salt

Preheat the oven to 210°F (100°C/Gas mark ¼).

Place the cherry tomatoes on a sheet pan (baking tray) lined with baking parchment. Add the confectioners' (icing) sugar, extra virgin olive oil, garlic clove, fresh thyme, and salt to taste, and cook for around 1 hour. Set aside.

Heat the milk in a pan, add the ricotta and Pecorino and leave to melt to make a soft cream. Add a handful of chopped fresh herbs to the cheese mixture and stir through.

Cook the pasta in plenty of lightly salted, boiling water, drain when al dente, and mix into the herby cream. Stir through the cherry tomatoes for the perfect contrast of flavor and color.

GEMELLI WITH CREAM OF PARMIGIANO AND LIME

The juicy citrus of the lime lends freshness to this dish, and makes even the simplest sauce something special.

20 min   10 min

SERVES 4

11 oz/320 g gemelli or mezze
   maniche
strips of zest and juice of 2 limes
generous ¾ cup (7 fl oz/200 ml)
   heavy (double) cream
3½ oz/100 g Parmigiano Reggiano,
   grated
pinch of finely chopped parsley
salt and freshly ground black
   pepper

Bring a pan of lightly salted water to the boil. Blanch the lime zest strips in the boiling water for 20 seconds and set aside.

Pour a little of the lime juice into the boiling water—putting the rest to one side—and cook the pasta according to the packet instructions.

In the meantime, gently heat the cream in a small saucepan together with the Parmigiano Reggiano, stirring well until combined and creamy. Add a few drops of lime juice to thicken, then put to one side.

Drain the gemelli when very al dente, reserving a little of the cooking water. Finish cooking the pasta in the pan with the Parmigiano cream for a couple of minutes, adding as much of the cooking water as needed for a creamy sauce.

Serve with a grinding of pepper, a pinch of chopped parsley, and garnish with the blanched lime zests.

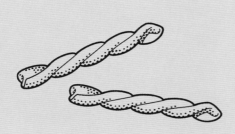

GEMELLI WITH PESTO ALLA TRAPANESE

The Genovese ships from the East landed in Trapani, where the sailors—finally on land—would eat pasta with a sauce of garlic and walnuts. The locals replaced the walnuts with almonds and tomato... *et voilà,* Pesto alla Trapanese was born.

20 min 10 min

SERVES 4

11 oz/320 g gemelli or fusilli
10 tomatoes, sliced
handful of basil leaves
6 cloves garlic
extra virgin olive oil, for grinding
   and frying
1½ oz/40 g blanched almonds,
   toasted and chopped
1½ oz/40 g fresh bread crumbs
salt and freshly ground black
   pepper

Grind the tomatoes in a pestle and mortar with the basil, garlic, and salt and pepper. When the sauce is nicely mixed, add a little oil and the chopped almonds and grind a little longer to incorporate.

Brown the bread crumbs in a little oil in a skillet (frying pan) for a few minutes until golden brown.

Cook the pasta in plenty of salted, boiling water according to the packet instructions. Drain when al dente, and toss with the tomato and almond pesto. Sprinkle with the bread crumbs and serve.

Tip
For a more robust flavor, you can substitute the bread crumbs with dots of salty, aged ricotta.

PENNE RIGATE ALLA NORMA

50 min   15 min

SERVES 4

11 oz/320 g penne rigate or mezze
    maniche
8¾ oz/250 g eggplant (aubergine),
    diced
all-purpose (plain) flour
3 tablespoons extra virgin olive oil,
    plus extra for frying
1¾ oz/50 g onion, chopped
1 clove garlic, peeled
2¼ lb/1 kg vine tomatoes, chopped
6 basil leaves, ripped
⅓ cup (1¾ oz/50 g) ricotta salata,
    grated
salt and freshly ground black
    pepper

Place the eggplant (aubergine) in a colander, sprinkle with salt, and leave for around 30 minutes until they discard all their liquids. Then toss the eggplant in flour to coat and fry in a skillet (frying pan) with plenty of oil for 3–5 minutes until browned.

Heat the oil in a pan over medium heat and brown the onion and the garlic clove for 5 minutes. Add the tomatoes, salt, and pepper and cook for around 10 minutes, then pass through a food mill. Add the fried eggplant cubes to the tomato sauce.

In the meantime, cook the pasta in plenty of salted, boiling water according to the packet instructions. Drain when al dente and coat with the sauce, adding the ripped basil. Serve sprinkled with the grated ricotta.

PENNE RIGATE ALL'ARRABBIATA

15 min   20 min

SERVES 4

11 oz/320 g penne rigate or
   tortiglioni
3 tablespoons extra virgin olive oil
2 cloves garlic, sliced
1 fresh red chili pepper, sliced (or
   use 1 dried chili pepper, see Tip)
1⅓ lb/600 g canned peeled
   tomatoes
¾ oz/20 g parsley, finely chopped
salt

Heat the oil in a pan over medium-high heat, and cook
the garlic and chili pepper for 2–3 minutes until browned,
taking care not to overcook.

Add the tomatoes and salt to taste, and continue cooking
over high heat for around 15 minutes, stirring occasionally
with a wooden spoon to break up the tomatoes.

In the meantime, cook the pasta in plenty of salted, boiling
water according to the packet instructions. Drain when al
dente, stir through the sauce, and garnish with a sprinkling
of chopped parsley.

Tip
If using a dried chili pepper, wear disposable gloves to
crumble it.

PASTA: FROM WHEAT TO SEMOLINA

Durum wheat semolina and water. In a single word: pasta.

In Italy, everyone eats pasta; in fact one in two Italians consider it their favorite food (on average in Italy, each person consumes 50 pounds/23 kilos of pasta per year). Only a quality product could have conquered the Italians in this way, and continue to capture their hearts and brighten their tables even today.

According to an ancient tradition which became law in 1967, in Italy dry pasta is made exclusively with durum wheat, allowing for a greater shelf life and yield. And given such a basic composition, it is clear that you can only obtain good pasta with quality durum wheat.

With its typical yellow color, semolina is obtained from the grinding of durum wheat grains, which are hard and translucent in structure. Mixed with water, the semolina then transforms into a dough with a tenacious structure, which guarantees the stability of the pasta shapes.

The quantity and quality of proteins contained in the durum wheat used, in addition to the manufacturing process and production techniques, contribute to determining the al dente quality of the pasta. The greater the amounts of protein, the better the body and consistency of the final product. For Italian pasta, the minimum quantity of protein required by law is at least 10.5 percent, but many Italian companies tend to produce pasta with a higher protein level.

When brought into contact with water, these proteins create gluten, which gives the pasta its "backbone," retaining and binding the starch. The greater the strength of the protein network, the tighter its mesh, and the less starch the pasta will lose during cooking.

HOW TO RECOGNIZE THE QUALITY OF PASTA

A good-quality pasta is characterized by a light yellow color, the result of the durum wheat semolina. An orange or brownish color indicates that the pasta has been subjected to a harsh drying process, which has burned the starches. And as the "look" is so important, upon careful visual inspection, there must be no microfractures (which can be seen by looking at the shape against the light), no black dots (due to the presence of impurities in the semolina), and no white dots (resulting from the imperfect hydration of the semolina). When properly produced, pasta should retain the fragrant smell of wheat.

During cooking, the starch must be released slowly to avoid the pasta becoming sticky. And, at the end of cooking, the pasta should maintain its elasticity so that, once removed from the boiling water and the hydration phase has ceased, it recompacts a little. If cooked al dente, it will offer some resistance to the bite, a pleasant hardness.

RIGATONI CACIO E PEPE

10 min   10 min

SERVES 4

11 oz/320 g rigatoni or mezze
    maniche
7 oz/200 g Pecorino Romano,
    grated
⅓ cup (3½ fl oz/100 ml) extra
    virgin olive oil
salt and freshly ground black
    pepper

Cook the pasta in plenty of salted, boiling water according to the packet instructions.

In the meantime, mix the grated Pecorino with the oil and 2–3 tablespoons of the pasta cooking water to loosen.

Drain when the pasta is al dente, and stir through the Pecorino mixture, adding black pepper to taste. Anything from a light dusting to an abundant grinding is fine—the important thing is it is freshly ground. Serve immediately.

RIGATONI WITH ARTICHOKES

20 min   20 min

SERVES 4

11 oz/320 g rigatoni or penne
    rigate
2¾ tablespoons extra virgin
    olive oil
4 artichokes, cleaned and cut
    into rounds
1 clove garlic, finely chopped
2 oz/60 g shallot, finely chopped
1 oz/30 g parsley, finely chopped
chili powder, to taste
3 tablespoons plus 1½ teaspoons
    white wine
3 tablespoons plus 1½ teaspoons
    vegetable broth (stock)
salt

Heat the oil in a pan over medium heat and cook the artichokes with the chopped garlic, shallot, parsley, and chili powder and salt to taste for 5 minutes.

Add the white wine and simmer until evaporated, about 3–4 minutes, then add the broth and cook for 10 minutes.

Cook the pasta in plenty of salted, boiling water according to the packet instructions. Drain when al dente, and toss with the artichoke sauce.

COQUILLETTES WITH PUMPKIN CREAM

20 min   20 min

SERVES 4

11 oz/320 g coquillettes or risoni
3 tablespoons extra virgin olive
   oil
1 onion, sliced
2 sprigs rosemary, leaves picked,
   plus extra, to garnish
24¾ oz/700 g pumpkin flesh, diced
7 oz/200 g potatoes, diced
6 cups (50 fl oz/1.5 liters)
   vegetable broth (stock)
salt and freshly ground black
   pepper

Heat the oil in a pan and cook the onion and rosemary for 5 minutes, until the onion is browned.

Add the pumpkin and the potatoes, leave to brown a little, then add the broth (stock). Add salt and pepper to taste, cook for 15 minutes until tender, reserve a little for garnish, then blend the remainder to a creamy purée.

Cook the pasta in plenty of salted, boiling water according to the packet instructions. Drain when al dente and pour into the pumpkin cream. Garnish with fresh rosemary and diced pumpkin.

SEDANINI WITH CREAM OF PORCINI, LEEKS, AND BLACK TRUFFLE

20 min   15 min

SERVES 4

11 oz/320 g sedanini or mezze
    maniche
4 tablespoons extra virgin olive oil
1 leek, cut into rounds
1 oz/30 g black truffle, chopped
7 oz/200 g porcini mushrooms,
    fresh or frozen, coarsely
    chopped
generous ¾ cup (7 fl oz/200 ml)
    vegetable broth (stock)
generous ¾ cup (7 fl oz/200 ml)
    cooking (single) cream
1¾ oz/50 g Parmigiano Reggiano,
    grated
2 tablespoons black truffle butter
1 tablespoon chopped parsley
salt and freshly ground black
    pepper

Heat the extra virgin olive oil in a saucepan and sauté the leek for 5 minutes until slightly golden. Add the truffle and porcini and continue sautéing for 2 minutes. Stir in the broth and cream, bring to a simmer for 7–8 minutes, then season with salt and pepper.

In the meantime, cook the pasta in plenty of salted, boiling water according to the packet instructions. Drain when al dente and mix with the sauce.

Stir through the Parmigiano, truffle butter, and parsley before serving.

TRUFFLE

This edible subterranean fungus, often difficult to find, grows underground near the roots of trees—particularly oaks—and has been celebrated since ancient times for its extraordinary flavor. During harvest, gatherers often use trained animals to catch the scent—the famous truffle dogs.

Jewels of Italian gastronomy, truffles are loved for their intense, decisive aroma. They add a distinctive note to any dish, making every bite an extraordinary culinary experience. There are different varieties of truffle, but the two that most commonly embellish the tables of gourmets and enthusiasts alike are white and black.

White truffle—*Tuber magnatum*—is considered the diamond of truffles, thanks to its penetrating aroma and delicate flavor. Commonly found in Piedmont and Tuscany, it is creamy white in color and has a wrinkled surface. In the kitchen it is often grated fresh over pasta, risotto, or even simpler dishes such as eggs.

Black truffle—*Tuber melanosporum*—also known as the winter truffle, has a firmer pulp and a more robust flavor. It grows in various Italian regions and develops in symbiosis with the roots of trees such as holm oak and hazelnut. Its color varies from dark brown to black, and it has a wrinkled and often irregular surface. It is commonly used in the preparation of sauces and often added, freshly sliced, to pasta dishes.

PIPE RIGATE WITH ARTICHOKES AND CREAM OF TALEGGIO

This dish acts as a melting pot for the tender, flavorsome artichokes and the sapidity of the Taleggio. The pipe rigate, with their dual opening, are the ideal shape to capture the sauce.

45 min   20 min

SERVES 4

11 oz/320 g pipe rigate or mezze maniche
2¾ tablespoons extra virgin olive oil
4 artichokes, cleaned and cut into rounds
1 clove garlic, finely chopped
1 tablespoon chopped parsley
3 tablespoons plus 1½ teaspoons dry white wine
3 tablespoons plus 1½ teaspoons vegetable broth (stock)
8¾ oz/250 g Taleggio
⅔ cup (5 fl oz/150 ml) milk, plus extra if needed
salt and freshly ground black pepper

Heat the oil in a pan and cook the artichokes with the chopped garlic and parsley for 5 minutes, adding salt and pepper to taste.

Add the white wine, leave to evaporate completely for 3–4 minutes, then add the broth (stock) and leave to cook for around 10 minutes.

In the meantime, remove the rind from the Taleggio and cut the cheese into cubes.

Put the milk in a small saucepan, bring to a boil, and add the cheese. Stir well until the Taleggio has melted and you are left with a smooth fondue. If necessary, dilute with more milk to reach the desired consistency, and add salt to taste. Keep warm.

Cook the pasta in plenty of salted, boiling water according to the packet instructions. Drain when al dente, and add to the pan with the artichokes. Cook for 2 minutes, then serve with the Taleggio fondue.

Tip
For a more delicate flavor, substitute the Taleggio with the same amount of Asiago cheese, taking care to choose one that is not over aged.

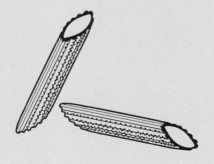

MEZZE MANICHE WITH CLAMS AND CHICKPEAS

Sweet is the night passed by the chickpeas as they soak. And as the sun rises, so the clams open in their oil, garlic, and parsley. The mezze maniche can't wait to dive into that sea of aromas.

30 min   11 min

SERVES 4

11 oz/320 g mezze maniche
  or coquillettes
¼ cup (2 fl oz/60 ml) extra virgin
  olive oil
1 clove garlic
1 fresh red chili pepper
1 cup (¾ oz/20 g) finely chopped
  parsley
28¼ oz/800 g clams, cleaned (see
  Tip)
1½ cups (8¾ oz/250 g) cooked
  chickpeas
4–5 basil leaves, cut into ribbons
salt and freshly ground black
  pepper

Heat half of the oil in a pan and brown the garlic clove, chili pepper, and parsley for 2 minutes. Add the clams and leave to open, about 4 minutes. Once opened, strain (and retain) the cooking juices, and discard some of the clam shells.

Crush the chickpeas with a fork (or blend for a creamier texture), softening the purée with a little clam cooking water and the remaining oil. Then season with a pinch of salt and a grinding of pepper.

Cook the pasta in plenty of salted, boiling water according to the packet instructions. Drain when al dente, and sauté in the pan with the clams and chickpea purée for a minute or two, then garnish with the basil.

Tips
This sauce is ideal for other forms of short pasta, such as rigatoni and penne rigate.

To clean clams, brush with a stiff brush to remove any impurities, then place them in a bowl of salted cold water for at least 20 minutes. Remove with a slotted spoon and rinse under cold running water. Discard any that are cracked or open. After cooking, discard any that remain closed.

MEZZE MANICHE WITH RED MULLET AND SAFFRON

40 min   15 min

SERVES 4

11 oz/320 g mezze maniche or
   penne rigate
2 tablespoons (1 oz/30 g) butter
½ celery stalk, diced
½ carrot, diced
¼ onion, diced
1 potato, cut into ¼-inch/
   ½-cm cubes
⅔ cup (5 fl oz/150 ml) heavy
   (double) cream
1 sachet saffron
1 tablespoon plus 1½ teaspoons
   extra virgin olive oil
1 sprig rosemary, leaves picked
   and chopped
8 small red mullet, scaled, filleted,
   and deboned
2 vine tomatoes, peeled,
   deseeded, and diced (see page
   26)
salt and freshly ground black
   pepper

Heat the butter in a pan and fry the celery, carrot, and onion together with the potato for 5 minutes. Add the cream and saffron, bring to the boil for a few minutes, add salt and pepper to taste, and keep warm off the heat.

In a separate pan, heat the oil over low heat and fry the rosemary for 2 minutes. Add the red mullet and brown quickly on both sides, starting with skin-side up. Remove from the heat and keep warm.

Cook the pasta in plenty of salted, boiling water according to the packet instructions. Drain when al dente and serve with the sauce, diced tomatoes, and red mullet fillets.

MEZZE PENNE WITH BABY SQUID ON A NAVY BEAN PURÉE

30 min   1 hour

SERVES 4

11 oz/320 g mezze penne or
    casarecce
5¼ oz/150 g dried navy (haricot)
    beans, soaked overnight
5¼ oz/150 g soffritto mix (finely
    diced celery stalk, carrot,
    and onion)
3 cloves garlic
3 sage leaves
3 tablespoons plus 1½ teaspoons
    extra virgin olive oil, plus extra
    for cooking and drizzling
1 sprig rosemary
1 sprig parsley
8¾ oz/250 g baby squid, cleaned
    and finely chopped (see Tip)
2 tablespoons plus 1½ teaspoons
    toasted pine nuts
salt and freshly ground black
    pepper

Rinse the beans and put them in a large pan with the soffritto mix, 1 clove of garlic, and 2 sage leaves. Cover with water, bring to a boil, and simmer for around 1 hour, gradually adding more water if needed. Add a little salt towards the end of the cooking time and put the pan to one side.

Heat the oil in a pan with 1 garlic clove, a sprig of rosemary, and a sage leaf for a few minutes. Strain the oil, add it to the beans, and blend to a purée.

In another pan, brown the parsley sprig and last unpeeled garlic clove in a little oil, then add the squid and cook for a few moments.

In the meantime, cook the pasta in plenty of salted, boiling water according to the packet instructions. Drain when al dente, then add to the pan with the squid and cook for 2 minutes.

Spread the bean purée on the plates, place the pasta in the middle, and garnish with a drizzle of oil and some toasted pine nuts. Add pepper to taste.

Tip
To clean squid and cuttlefish, remove the skin from the sac and separate the tentacles from the body; dispose of the interior. Remove the beak from the center of the tentacles and the eyes, and discard.

FARFALLE "MARE E MONTI"

30 min   10 min

SERVES 4

11 oz/320 g farfalle or penne
  rigate
3 tablespoons plus 1½ teaspoons
  extra virgin olive oil
1 tablespoon finely chopped
  parsley
2 cloves garlic (1 whole,
  1 chopped)
17¾ oz/500 g clams, cleaned (see
  page 57)
3 tablespoons plus 1½ teaspoons
  white wine
10½ oz/300 g cultivated
  mushrooms, washed
salt and freshly ground black
  pepper

Heat half of the oil in a pan and fry half of the chopped parsley and 1 whole clove of garlic for 2 minutes. Then add the clams and the white wine, cover, and cook until the clams are open, 3–4 minutes. Once open, discard some of the shells and the garlic, and strain and reserve the cooking liquid.

Heat the remaining oil in a pan with the chopped garlic clove and the remaining parsley, add the mushrooms, and sauté everything for 2 minutes over high heat, adding salt and pepper to taste. Add the clams and the cooking liquid to the mushrooms and, if necessary, leave the liquid to thicken a little.

In the meantime, cook the pasta in plenty of salted, boiling water according to the packet instructions. Drain when al dente, add to the pan with the clams, sauté quickly, and serve.

FARFALLE WITH FRESH TUNA AND TAGGIASCA OLIVES

30 min   10 min

SERVES 4

11 oz/320 g farfalle or rigatoni
6 tablespoons extra virgin olive oil
3½ oz/100 g leek, finely chopped
3½ oz/100 g carrot, finely chopped
3½ oz/100 g celery stalk, finely
   chopped
21¼ oz/600 g tomatoes, peeled,
   deseeded, and diced (see page
   26)
1¾ oz/50 g Taggiasca olives, pitted
8¾ oz/250 g fresh tuna, cut into
   1-inch/2.5-cm cubes
3 sprigs marjoram, leaves picked
salt and freshly ground black
   pepper

Heat 3 tablespoons of oil in a pan with the leek, carrot, and celery, and cook for 3 minutes. Add the tomatoes and a pinch of salt and cook for 5 minutes, then add the olives to the sauce.

Cook the pasta in plenty of salted, boiling water according to the packet instructions.

In the meantime, sauté the tuna in a separate pan with the remaining oil over high heat for a couple of minutes until pink. Add salt and pepper, then add the tuna to the tomato sauce.

Drain the pasta when al dente, and serve with the sauce and a sprinkling of marjoram leaves.

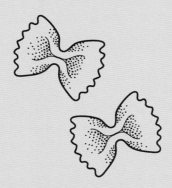

FUSILLI WITH ASPARAGUS AND TUNA

15 min   10 min

SERVES 4

11 oz/320 g fusilli or penne rigate
4 tablespoons extra virgin olive oil
1 shallot, finely sliced
5¼ oz/150 g asparagus, cleaned
    and cut into ¼-inch/5-mm
    rounds (keep the tips to one
    side)
5¼ oz/150 g tuna packed in oil,
    drained
2 tablespoons finely chopped
    parsley
grated Parmigiano Reggiano, to
    garnish (optional)
salt and freshly ground black
    pepper

Heat the oil in a pan and gently fry the shallot for 5 minutes. Add the asparagus rounds and cook until browned, adding 1 tablespoon of water to aid the cooking process. After a few minutes, add the asparagus tips, the drained tuna, parsley, and, if necessary, a pinch of salt and pepper.

In the meantime, cook the pasta in plenty of salted, boiling water according to the packet instructions, then drain when al dente and add to the sauce.

If you like, garnish with a light sprinkling of Parmigiano Reggiano and serve.

CASARECCE WITH ANCHOVIES AND SPICY BREAD CRUMBS

10 min   10 min

SERVES 4

11 oz/320 g casarecce or penne
    lisce
¼ cup (2 fl oz/60 ml) extra virgin
    olive oil
4 salt-packed anchovies, rinsed
    and deboned
4 tablespoons fresh bread crumbs
pinch of hot chili powder
salt

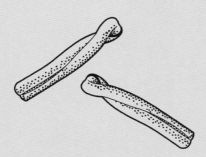

Heat half of the oil in a pan on low heat. When hot, add the anchovies and cook for a few minutes until broken up.

In the meantime, heat another pan with the remaining oil on medium heat, add the bread crumbs and chili powder, and leave to toast for 2–3 minutes, or until lightly golden in color.

In the meantime, cook the pasta in plenty of salted, boiling water according to the packet instructions. Drain when al dente, and serve with the anchovies and the toasted bread crumbs.

DITALONI RIGATI WITH MUSSELS, POTATOES, AND SAFFRON

20 min 10 min

SERVES 4

11 oz/320 g ditaloni rigati
    or coquillettes
3 tablespoons extra virgin olive oil,
    plus extra for drizzling
17¾ oz/500 g mussels, cleaned
    (see Tip)
1 bay leaf
1 clove garlic, peeled and whole
⅓ cup (3½ fl oz/100 ml) white wine
1 sachet saffron
5¾ oz/160 g potatoes, diced
1 tablespoon chopped parsley
salt and freshly ground black
    pepper

Heat the oil in a low, wide pan and add the mussels with the bay leaf, the whole garlic clove, and the wine. Cover and leave to cook over high heat until the mussels are open, about 4–5 minutes. At this point, discard some of the shells, strain the cooking liquid, and dissolve the saffron in the strained liquid.

Cook the pasta and potatoes together in plenty of salted, boiling water according to the pasta packet instructions. Drain while still very al dente and finish cooking in the pan with the mussels and saffron liquid. Sprinkle with the chopped parsley and serve with a grinding of pepper and a drizzle of fresh oil.

Tip
Clean the mussels under cold running water, scrubbing them with a stiff brush to get rid of any impurities, and removing the beard. Discard any that are cracked or open. After cooking, discard any that remain closed.

THE SECRET TO COOKING PASTA "AL DENTE"

Pasta cooked "al dente" (literally "to the tooth") represents the standard taste of Italians, both at home and in restaurants. Once cooked, the pasta should display a certain strength, or rather a certain resistance to chewing, and preserve its elasticity. If it is sticky or too soft, it is not "al dente." Furthermore, its texture should be as uniform as possible—it should not be soft on the outside and hard inside.

During the pasta cooking process, the water gradually penetrates the external surface of the pasta to reach the inside, hydrating it and making it swell. The cooking process is a vital step in creating a successful dish: if cooked badly, even the best quality pasta can give a poor result.

The classic cooking method requires water and coarse salt. The general rule for the proportions is thus: 25 oz/7 g of coarse salt in 2 pints/1 liter of water for every 3½ oz/100 g of pasta. These quantities may vary slightly, depending on taste, local customs, and the requirements of the cook—but always following the principle that there must be enough water for the pasta to "float" sufficiently well, and the water should return quickly to the boil after cooling on contact with the pasta. The boiling temperature is influenced by various factors, such as altitude and hardness of the water; it is important to remember that by using a lid on the pan, the water will come to the boil more quickly due to less dispersion of heat.

During the first cooking phase of the pasta, it is a good idea to stir it with a wooden spoon to avoid it sticking to the bottom of the pan. A good rule of thumb is to check the cooking time for your chosen shape, then set a clock or timer for the required duration, but be ready to taste it a minute before the end of the indicated time. If you have to choose between draining a little early or a little late, drain early, always keeping a little cooking water to one side in case it is needed later. If the pasta is topped with a sauce, you can drain while al dente. If you wish to stir the pasta into the pan containing the sauce, drain it a couple of minutes early so that it continues cooking in the sauce, which avoids the risk of overcooking.

LINGUINE WITH CUTTLEFISH INK

10 min   12 min

SERVES 4

11 oz/320 g linguine or casarecce
2¼ tablespoons extra virgin
    olive oil
1 clove garlic, peeled and whole
1 oz/30 g parsley, finely chopped
1 fresh red chili pepper, finely
    chopped
14 oz/400 g San Marzano
    tomatoes, deseeded and thinly
    sliced
1 tablespoon cuttlefish ink
salt

Cook the pasta in plenty of salted, boiling water according to the packet instructions.

In the meantime, heat the oil in a pan with the whole garlic clove, then add the parsley (keep a pinch to one side for the garnish) and the chili pepper. Fry for 1 minute, then add the tomatoes. Cook for a further 1 minute, then add the cuttlefish ink and one ladleful of pasta cooking water. Reduce the heat to low and cook for 2–3 minutes until reduced slightly, adding salt to taste.

Drain the pasta when al dente and pour into the pan. Sauté everything together for a minute or two, add a sprinkling of parsley, and serve.

LINGUINE WITH SEAFOOD

30 min 12 min

SERVES 4

11 oz/320 g linguine or
  Spaghetti n. 5
2¾ tablespoons extra virgin olive
  oil
1 clove garlic, finely chopped
1 tablespoon finely chopped
  parsley
1 sprig basil, coarsely chopped
14 oz/400 g mussels, cleaned
  (see page 70)
14 oz/400 g clams, cleaned
  (see page 57)
⅔ cup (5 fl oz/150 ml) white wine
3½ oz/100 g squid, cleaned (see
  page 60) and cut into rings
4 small cuttlefish, cleaned (see
  page 60) and cut into rings
4 langoustines
4 shrimp (prawn) tails
5¼ oz/150 g tomatoes, deseeded
  and sliced
salt and freshly ground
  black pepper

Heat the oil in a pan with the garlic, parsley, and basil for a minute or two. Add the mussels, clams, and white wine. Cover, and wait for the molluscs to open, 4–5 minutes, then remove from the pan, discard around three-quarters of the shells, and put the mussels and clams in a bowl.

In the same pan, cook the squid with the cuttlefish, whole langoustines, shrimp (prawn) tails, and tomatoes. Leave to brown for a few minutes, then add the mussels and clams and season to taste. Cook for 5–7 minutes; the sauce should still be rather liquid.

Cook the pasta in plenty of salted, boiling water according to the packet instructions. Drain when al dente, add to the pan with the seafood sauce, and cook for a couple of minutes before serving.

PIPE RIGATE WITH SHRIMP AND TOMATO

30 min   15 min

SERVES 4

11 oz/320 g pipe rigate or fusilli
16 raw shrimp (prawns)
5 tablespoons extra virgin olive oil
1 small red onion, chopped
1 tablespoon cornstarch
　(cornflour)
2 tablespoons brandy
1 tablespoon tomato paste
　(purée)
4 ripe red tomatoes, diced
chopped parsley, to garnish
salt and freshly ground black
　pepper

Clean and shell the shrimp (prawns), keeping the heads and shells. Cut the flesh into pieces and put to one side.

Heat 3 tablespoons of oil in a pan over medium-low heat and gently fry the onion for 5 minutes. Add the shrimp heads and shells and quickly toast. Add the cornstarch (cornflour) and cook for 1 minute, then add the brandy and flambé the alcohol. Add the tomato paste (purée), 2 ladlefuls of water, and leave to simmer for a few minutes. Strain, and put the liquid to one side.

Heat the remaining oil in a pan and sauté the shrimp for a few minutes. Add the tomatoes and leave to cook for 2–3 minutes. Season to taste.

In the meantime, cook the pasta in plenty of salted, boiling water according to the packet instructions. Drain when al dente, add to the pan with the shrimp and strained liquid, and sauté in the sauce for a couple of minutes, completing with a sprinkling of chopped parsley.

RISONI WITH RED SHRIMP, ORANGE, AND ASPARAGUS

Red shrimp (prawns), elevated by the asparagus, the bitterness of the citrus fruit, and the bright saffron, come together with the risoni to create something new, bringing with it a dream of summer.

50 min   35 min

SERVES 4

11 oz/320 g risoni
5¼ oz/150 g red shrimp (prawns)
5¼ oz/150 g soffritto mix (finely
    diced celery stalk, carrot, and
    onion)
4 asparagus, cleaned and
    trimmed
grated zest of 1 orange
extra virgin olive oil, for
    marinating and frying
3 sprigs wild fennel
2 shallots, chopped
⅓ cup (3½ fl oz/100 ml) white wine
1 sachet of saffron
1 tablespoon plus 1 teaspoon
    (¾ oz/20 g) butter, cold
1 oz/30 g Parmigiano Reggiano,
    grated
salt and freshly ground black
    pepper

Clean and shell the red shrimp (prawns), keeping the heads and shells to one side for preparing the broth: fill a saucepan with 6⅓ pints/3 liters of water and add the shrimp heads and shells, the soffritto mix, and the asparagus trimmings; leave to cook for around 20 minutes.

Marinate the shrimp for 15 minutes with the orange zest, salt, pepper, some extra virgin olive oil, and the wild fennel. When ready, heat a drizzle of oil in a nonstick pan and fry the shrimp with some salt and pepper. Put to one side.

Toast the risoni in a pan with some oil and the shallots, add a little white wine, and cook, adding the broth as you would for a risotto. Dissolve the saffron in ½ cup (4 fl oz/120 ml) of hot broth and add to the risoni about two-thirds of the way through the cooking time (after 6–8 minutes). Once the risoni is cooked, stir in the cold butter and Parmigiano.

Prepare a pan of boiling water and blanch the asparagus quickly, then transfer to a skillet (frying pan) and fry in oil for a few seconds.

Use a square food mold to serve: fill it completely with the risoni, trying to create a uniform cube on the plate. Complete the risoni cube with the asparagus and the hot shrimp.

Tip
If you wish, you can add a few drops of parsley oil to the dish before serving, to add color and aroma: Wash ¾ oz/20 g parsley, blanch in salted, boiling water for 1 minute, then cool in water, squeeze, and blend with 1¾ oz/50 g extra virgin olive oil. The resulting oil should be rather liquid and a brilliant green in color.

PENNE RIGATE WITH SARDINES

Some love it for the intense flavor of the sardines, some for the unmistakable aroma of wild fennel, and others for the hint of sweet and sour given by the golden raisins (sultanas). But it's the penne rigate that is the genuine and decisive heart and soul of this dish, one of the most loved in Sicilian tradition.

20 min   15 min

SERVES 4

11 oz/320 g penne rigate or penne lisce

3 tablespoons plus 1½ teaspoons extra virgin olive oil

3 cloves garlic, peeled and whole

pinch of saffron, diluted with a drop of water

7 oz/200 g fresh sardines, cleaned, filleted, and deboned

3 oz/80 g anchovies, rinsed and deboned

1½ teaspoons chopped parsley

1 onion, finely chopped

2 sprigs wild fennel, chopped

3 tablespoons golden raisins (sultanas), soaked in lukewarm water for 20 minutes, then drained

4 tablespoons pine nuts

salt and freshly ground black pepper

Put 2 tablespoons of oil, 2 whole garlic cloves, a few tablespoons of cold water, and the saffron in a large skillet (frying pan) and season with salt and pepper to taste. Cook over medium heat for about 4 minutes, then add the sardines and continue cooking for 5 minutes. Remove from the heat, discard the garlic cloves, and set aside.

Crush the anchovies using a pestle and mortar, together with the parsley and a ladleful of warm water.

Heat the remaining oil in a pan until hot, then add the remaining garlic clove and the finely chopped onion. Fry until the onion is browned, about 5 minutes, then add the wild fennel, golden raisins (sultanas), pine nuts, and anchovy and parsley paste. Cook over moderate heat for 5 minutes.

In the meantime, cook the pasta in plenty of salted, boiling water according to the packet instructions. Drain the pasta when al dente, mix with the sauce and sardines, and serve.

Tip

A typical Sicilian dish, pasta with sardines is prepared differently in different areas of the island. In Palermo, the dish is completed with a sprinkling of fresh bread crumbs sautéed in a nonstick pan with a few tablespoons of oil.

PENNE RIGATE ALLA PUTTANESCA

30 min   10 min

SERVES 4

11 oz/320 g penne rigate or
   rigatoni
2 tablespoons extra virgin olive oil
2 cloves garlic, sliced
dried or fresh red chili pepper,
   sliced
4 tablespoons salt-packed capers,
   rinsed and coarsely chopped
1 oz/25 g oil-packed anchovy
   fillets
17¾ oz/500 g canned peeled or
   crushed tomatoes
1¾ oz/50 g pitted black olives,
   halved or cut into rounds
¾ oz/20 g parsley, finely chopped
salt

Heat the oil in a pan over low heat and fry the garlic with
the chili pepper for 2 minutes, taking care not to overcook.
Once browned, add the capers and anchovy fillets, and
continue cooking over low heat for 2 minutes.

Turn up the heat to high and add the tomatoes. Add
salt if necessary and cook for around 5 minutes, stirring
occasionally, then add the olives.

In the meantime, cook the pasta in plenty of salted, boiling
water according to the packet instructions. Drain when al
dente, stir through the sauce, and garnish with a sprinkling
of chopped parsley.

PENNETTE WITH EGGPLANT AND SWORDFISH

30 min   20 min

SERVES 4

11 oz/320 g pennette or fusilli
10½ oz/300 g eggplant
   (aubergines), diced
all-purpose (plain) flour, for
   dusting
vegetable oil, for frying
2 tablespoons extra virgin olive oil
1 clove garlic, chopped
7 oz/200 g swordfish, diced
¾ cup (6 fl oz/175 ml) white wine
8¾ oz/250 g cherry tomatoes, cut
   into wedges
½ oz/10 g basil leaves, ripped, plus
   extra leaves to garnish
salt and freshly ground black
   pepper

Dust the eggplant (aubergine) with flour, and fry in a skillet (frying pan) in plenty of hot vegetable oil for 5 minutes. Once browned, drain on paper towels.

Cook the pasta in plenty of salted, boiling water according to the packet instructions.

Heat the extra virgin olive oil in a pan with the garlic clove for a minute or two to flavor, then add the swordfish and salt to taste. Leave to brown on high heat for 30 seconds, then add the white wine and leave to evaporate for 3–4 minutes.

Reduce the heat to low, add the cherry tomatoes and some black pepper and leave to cook for 3–4 minutes. Add the fried eggplants and ripped basil leaves, loosening the sauce with a little of the pasta cooking water, if necessary, and leave to cook for 2 minutes.

Drain the pasta when al dente, add to the sauce, cook for a couple of minutes, and complete with a few basil leaves.

GEMELLI WITH PROSCIUTTO AND BROCCOLI

 10 min   15 min

SERVES 4

10½ oz/300 g gemelli or conchiglie rigate
3 tablespoons extra virgin olive oil
5¼ oz/150 g Prosciutto di Parma, diced
1 sage leaf
7 oz/200 g broccoli, cleaned and broken into florets (cut the stalks into rounds)
2 tablespoons (1 oz/30 g) butter
grated zest and juice of ½ unwaxed lemon
salt

Heat 2 tablespoons of oil in a pan and gently brown the Prosciutto with the sage for 2–3 minutes.

Add around 2 pints/1 liter of water and bring to the boil. Add a pinch of salt, then throw in the pasta, broccoli, butter, lemon juice, and remaining oil. Leave to cook for around 10 minutes over a low heat, so the pasta absorbs the water slowly.

If necessary, add a little more water every so often, stirring everything well. When cooked, sprinkle over a little grated lemon zest and serve.

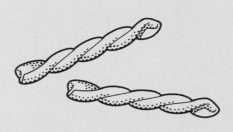

PROSCIUTTO DI PARMA

Prosciutto di Parma PDO (Protected Designation of Origin) is one of Italy's most celebrated gastronomic delights, recognized worldwide for its superior quality and unmistakable flavor. It is the result of a centuries-old artisanal production process handed down from generation to generation by master makers who mature the product in the hilly area of Parma. The PDO label is an indication of its authenticity and geographical origin.

It is made with pork legs, which, once washed and dried, are salted by hand and then subjected to a maturing period that varies from twelve to thirty-six months. The sea wind which blows through the surrounding hills completes the maturing process.

Prosciutto di Parma can be enjoyed alone as an appetizer alongside slices of melon or fresh figs, or with flakes of Parmigiano Reggiano. It is also found in many Italian dishes, such as pasta, pizza, focaccia, and salads. A pillar of traditional and gourmet Italian cuisine, Prosciutto di Parma is now recognized and enjoyed all over the world.

SPAGHETTI ALLA CARBONARA

10 min   15 min   5

SERVES 4

11 oz/320 g Spaghetti n. 5
    or mezze maniche
4 egg yolks
3½ oz/100 g Pecorino Romano,
    grated
5¼ oz/150 g guanciale (pork cheek
    lard), cut into strips or diced
salt and freshly ground black
    pepper

In a mixing bowl, beat the egg yolks with a pinch of salt
and 1 tablespoon of grated Pecorino.

Heat the guanciale slowly in a large, shallow pan over
medium heat for a few minutes until lightly browned.

Cook the pasta in plenty of salted, boiling water according
to the packet instructions. Drain when al dente, retaining
1 cup of the cooking water.

Put the pasta into the pan with the guanciale, sauté for
a few moments, then turn off the heat. Add the beaten
egg yolks and 1 ladleful of cooking water and stir for around
30 seconds.

Stir through the remaining Pecorino and some freshly
ground black pepper and serve immediately.

RIGATONI ALL'AMATRICIANA

Who could forget Gregory Peck and Audrey Hepburn riding around the streets of Rome on a Vespa in *Roman Holiday*? Beautiful and iconic, a little like rigatoni all'Amatriciana, an ambassador of Italian cuisine throughout the world.

15 min   15 min

SERVES 4

11 oz/320 g rigatoni or penne lisce
5¼ oz/150 g guanciale (pork cheek lard), cut into strips
3½ oz/100 g onion, thinly sliced
1 red chili pepper, thinly sliced
3 tablespoons plus 1½ teaspoons extra virgin olive oil
4 ripe tomatoes, peeled, deseeded, and diced (see page 26)
1½ oz/40 g Pecorino Romano, grated
salt and freshly ground black pepper

Put the guanciale and a splash of water in a pan on high heat and allow the fat to render. Add the onion and chili pepper with the oil, and cook for 5 minutes.

Add the tomatoes and cook for 10 minutes. If necessary, add a pinch of salt and a sprinkling of pepper.

In the meantime, cook the pasta in plenty of salted, boiling water. Drain when al dente, and garnish with the sauce and grated Pecorino. Stir well and serve hot.

Tip
When out of season, you can substitute the fresh tomatoes with the same quantity of canned peeled tomatoes.

RIGATONI WITH RAGÙ ALLA NAPOLETANA

It is said that throughout Naples on Sunday mornings, people get up early to make ragù. At the end of the meal, when the plates are empty, it is simply obligatory to soak up whatever's left with a piece of bread. Ragù was traditionally served as a second course, after the pasta.

20 min   2 h 5 min

SERVES 4

11 oz/320 g rigatoni or penne lisce
⅓ cup (3½ fl oz/100 ml) extra
    virgin olive oil
7 oz/200 g onions, chopped
6 basil leaves
2 pork spare ribs, cut into pieces
7 oz/200 g lean beef steak, cut
    into pieces
7 oz/200 g stewing beef, cut into
    pieces
⅔ cup (5 fl oz/150 ml) red wine
2¼ lb/1 kg canned crushed
    tomatoes
salt and freshly ground black
    pepper

Heat the oil in a pan over medium heat, add the onion, basil, spare ribs, lean beef, and stewing beef, and cook for 5 minutes. Pour in the red wine and, when it has evaporated, add the crushed tomatoes and leave to cook for at least 2 hours, stirring occasionally. Adjust salt and pepper to taste.

In the meantime, cook the pasta in plenty of salted, boiling water. Drain when al dente, then transfer to the pan of sauce and cook for a couple of minutes before serving.

Tip
Ragù alla Napoletana, like all meat ragù, requires very gentle and long cooking. The tomato sauce must slowly absorb all the flavors of the meat. Traditionally, in Campania this dish is cooked on Sunday.

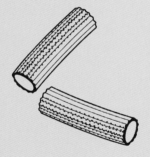

MEZZE MANICHE WITH RAGÙ AND EGGPLANT

The generous flavors of the beef and veal, the balanced acidity of the tomato, and the spicy crunch of the eggplant (aubergine) make this dish the perfect example of equilibrium. A recipe for the holidays.

 30 min   55 min

SERVES 4

11 oz/320 g mezze maniche
  or penne rigate
1 tablespoon plus 1 teaspoon
  (¾ oz/20 g) butter
3 tablespoons plus 1½ teaspoons
  extra virgin olive oil
1¾ oz/50 g Prosciutto di Parma,
  chopped
½ onion, sliced
7 oz/200 g lean beef,
  cut into pieces
3½ oz/100 g lean veal,
  cut into pieces
⅓ cup (3½ fl oz/100 ml)
  dry white wine
21¼ oz/600 g canned crushed
  tomatoes
1 eggplant (aubergine),
  peeled and diced
2¼ oz/60 g Parmigiano Reggiano,
  grated
salt and freshly ground
  black pepper

Heat the butter and half of the oil in a pan over medium heat. Add the Prosciutto and onion and cook for 5 minutes until browned.

Add the beef and veal, increase the heat to high, and cook until the meat is browned, about 5 minutes, then add the wine. When the wine is completely evaporated, 3–4 minutes, add the crushed tomatoes and enough water to cover the meat. Season with salt and pepper and bring to the boil. Cover and continue cooking over a moderate flame for around 40 minutes.

A few minutes before the end of the ragù cooking time, sauté the eggplant (aubergine) in a pan with the remaining oil for 5 minutes, then add it to the ragù.

In the meantime, cook the pasta in plenty of lightly salted, boiling water. Drain when al dente and serve with the ragù and a dusting of grated Parmigiano.

Tip
For a more delicate dish, substitute the eggplant (aubergine) with 2 zucchini (courgettes). You can also flavor the dish with fresh thyme before serving, to lend an air of freshness to the ragù.

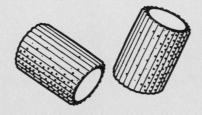

TRADITIONAL SEDANINI TIMBALE

Pasta timbale has been around since the dawn of time.
A dish to leave your guests open-mouthed.

2 hours   65 min

SERVES 4

8¾ oz/250 g sedanini or penne
    rigate
2 tablespoons extra virgin olive oil
5¼ oz/150 g soffritto mix (finely
    diced celery stalk, carrot, and
    onion)
1 bay leaf
3½ oz/100 g ground (minced) pork
4¼ oz/120 g ground (minced) beef
1¾ oz/50 g chicken livers, cleaned
    and diced
¾ oz/20 g bacon, chopped
⅓ cup (3 fl oz/80 ml) red wine
4 tablespoons tomato paste
    (purée)
1¾ oz/50 g Parmigiano Reggiano,
    grated
1 egg, beaten
salt and freshly ground black
    pepper

FOR THE SHORTCRUST PASTRY
8¾ oz/250 g butter,
    softened
6⅓ oz/180 g superfine (caster)
    sugar
2 eggs
17¾ oz/500 g all-purpose (plain)
    flour, plus extra for dusting

Prepare the shortcrust pastry by mixing the softened butter with the sugar. Add the eggs, mix well, then add the flour and a pinch of salt. Use your hands to knead and bring the dough together without handling it too much. Then roll in plastic wrap (cling film) and leave to rest in the refrigerator for at least 1 hour.

Heat a drizzle of oil in a pan over medium heat and cook the soffritto mix and bay leaf for 5 minutes until the vegetables have browned. Increase the heat and add the pork, beef, livers, and bacon, and cook for 5 minutes. Once browned, add salt, pepper, and the red wine, and cook until the wine has evaporated completely, 3–4 minutes. Reduce the heat to low and add the tomato paste (purée). Cover with 2 cups (17 fl oz/500 ml) water and leave to simmer for 1 hour.

On a floured surface, roll out two-thirds of the pastry with a rolling pin until it is around ⅙ inch (4 mm) thick and use it to line a cake tin around 10–11 inches (26–28 cm) in diameter. Use the remaining pastry to make a disk as thick as the first as a top for the cake tin.

Preheat the oven to 350°F (180°C/Gas Mark 4).

Cook the pasta in plenty of salted, boiling water according to the packet instructions, but drain a few minutes before the cooking time indicated, so it is very al dente. Combine with the ragù and Parmigiano, then pour into the pastry-lined cake tin and cover with the pastry lid, sealing the edges well.

Brush the top with beaten egg and cook in the oven for around 20 minutes, or until the surface is nicely golden and crunchy.

Tip
Serve the timbale with a fondue of Parmigiano Reggiano: Melt 5¼ oz/150 g grated Parmigiano with the same amount of cream over low heat, let cool slightly, then blend well.

PASTA E FAGIOLI

20 min   85 min

SERVES 4

4¼ oz/120 g ditalini or risoni
5¼ oz/150 g lardo (back fat)
1 clove garlic, peeled and whole
1 onion, chopped
2¼ lb/1 kg fresh cranberry
    (borlotti) beans (or 17¾ oz/
    500 g canned cranberry/borlotti
    beans)
⅓ cup plus 1 tablespoon (3½ fl
    oz/100 ml) white wine
6½ cups (50 fl oz/1.5 liters) meat
    broth (stock)
8¾ oz/250 g red potatoes, peeled
1 sprig rosemary, chopped, plus
    extra to garnish
1 sprig parsley, chopped, plus
    extra to garnish
2 tablespoons (1 oz/30 g) butter
4 slices bread, toasted and
    brushed with garlic
salt and freshly ground black
    pepper

Heat the lardo in a pan over medium heat with the garlic clove, onion, and cranberry (borlotti) beans. Cook for 5 minutes, then add the white wine and simmer until evaporated, 3–4 minutes. Add the broth (stock) and salt to taste, then add the potatoes and leave to cook for around 1 hour until tender. Transfer one-third of the beans and the potatoes to a blender and blend to a purée. Set aside.

Add the pasta to the pan, and cook for around 15 minutes, then add the purée to the pan with the rosemary, parsley and butter.

Serve in individual bowls, garnished with rosemary, parsley, and a sprinkling of black pepper, and accompanied by slices of toasted bread brushed with garlic.

TORTIGLIONI ALLA GRICIA

10 min 10 min

SERVES 4

11 oz/320 g tortiglioni or
  mezze maniche
4 tablespoons extra virgin olive oil
8¾ oz/250 g guanciale (pork
  cheek lard), cut into pieces
1 fresh red chili pepper, finely
  chopped
2 oz/60 g Pecorino Romano,
  grated
salt and freshly ground
  black pepper

Cook the pasta in plenty of salted, boiling water according to the packet instructions.

In the meantime, heat the oil in a wide pan over medium heat. Add the guanciale and chili pepper and fry for 3 minutes.

Drain the pasta when al dente, pour into the pan with the guanciale and mix well, adding the Pecorino Romano and freshly ground black pepper to taste.

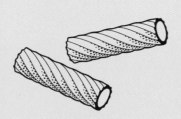

GOURMET

MEALS

FLAVOR AND PASSION

If you have seen the 2010 film *Eat, Pray, Love*, you will remember Julia Roberts' exquisite pleasure at eating a plate of spaghetti with tomato and basil in large forkfuls. Contemplating her expression of joy, it may have occurred to you that the human and the divine are not so distant after all.

If you can imagine it, then you can also taste it. It is a crescendo of the senses—you observe it, you smell it, you touch it, you possess it—and it is also a seduction of the mind. Pasta is form and substance, it is a culture that speaks to the stomach while elevating the spirit, a sort of philosophical viaticum to something better; a passe-partout to new experiences and a richer existence. Italians embrace it so intensely that they talk about it at the table just as much as they do in the kitchen.

It's a little like what happened to those young people in eighteenth- and nineteenth-century Europe who took part in the long Grand Tour. Inspired to travel by a desire to complete their cultural education, they were able to satisfy the curiosity stirred by tales and articles heard and read, long before the invention of the Internet and social media. Once in Italy, they encountered situations that, while perhaps confusing, also aroused amazement and wonder. As was the case for the German poet Heinrich Heine, who, in his book *Pictures of Travel*, wrote that "Italian cuisine, seasoned with passion, garnished with humor, but still ideally sighing, reflects the entire character of the beautiful Italian women.

Everything swims in oil, lazily and tenderly, and warbles sweet Rossini melodies and cries with the scent of onion and desire! But you have to eat macaroni with your fingers, and then it's called: Beatrice."

The possibility of encountering the unknown is, after all, the very essence of travel. You can get to know Italy through pasta. And through pasta, Italy travels the world and brings outside influences home, opening the way to new interpretations. We like to think that the plot of *A Room with a View* would have taken a very different turn if Lucy Honeychurch, a shy young lady from the English bourgeoisie traveling in Italy, and George Emerson, a young romantic and nonconformist, had enjoyed an inviting dish of linguine with garlic, oil, chili, bottarga, and lemon instead of cucumber and caviar sandwiches during their famous picnic on the hills above Florence.

The eternal conflict between reason and feeling can be quickly resolved by choosing pasta in its best version in terms of raw material, color, thickness, elasticity, tone, cooking resistance, and ability to retain sauce and, therefore, retain the high-quality taste. Hence the merit of the bronze dies, which draw micro-incisions, grooves, or special curvatures on the surface of the pasta, bringing out the best features of each shape and thereby enhancing the dish as a whole. The Barilla bronze-drawn gourmet pasta range underlines the character of the blend of grains, whose body and intense roughness are also stylistic and identifying features. Easily recognizable thanks to their beautiful amber yellow color, they are ideal for those who love a full bite and flavor.

Bronze-drawn pastas capture a greater quantity of sauce and, having significant flavor and consistency, stand up well in union with ingredients with a strong personality. So, leafing through the pages of this chapter, you may be surprised by the encounter between a classic Cacio e Pepe and the sweet-iodine notes of red shrimp (prawns), the pairing of caper flowers with coffee, or how the pulpy persuasiveness of langoustine unites with a burst of the surly flavor of bottarga. You will be amazed at the combination of a strong blue cheese and the various shades of natural sweetness that zucchini (courgettes), carrots, and cherry tomatoes can bring, and at the vibrant freshness that Nordic dill, along with the spicy complicity of ginger, can give to smoked salmon. The excellence of Italian food and wine, told through extraordinary native ingredients, is a heritage that is appreciated and loved throughout the world.

Any passion that remains alive is one that is continually fuelled. True passion brings with it study, the need for in-depth analysis, the desire for improvement. Gualtiero Marchesi, the greatest exponent of new Italian cuisine, maintained that gastronomic Italy is indeed the home of simplicity, but added that without awareness and professionalism it risked abandoning itself to improvisation and simplism. Studying is a

commitment that requires a firm will and time, but which becomes easy if you have passion. This is what binds the food enthusiasts frequenting the Chelsea Market or Union Square Greenmarket in New York, or those who meet in London at Borough Market, a few steps from the Thames, or at the Broadway Market in the East End; in fact anyone in any country who is willing to travel miles to find genuine, characteristic, and unusual products. Once back home they study the most suitable preparations for the ingredients found with such ardor, leafing through recipe books and consulting with gourmet friends. Finally, they also take care of the mise en place, thoughtfully choosing the wines to pair with the pasta and warmly welcoming their guests.

Daring new recipes means pushing into rarely explored terrain, seeking alternative trajectories of flavor. Those who love food observe the mastery of chefs, capturing their indispensable secrets. Each pasta shape must be the protagonist, each ingredient must add something without dominating the others, while at the same time maintaining its own identity in a subtle game of connections and references that finds fulfilment in a brand-new dish. It is a natural choice for those held up by the wings of passion, for those with the curiosity and patience to learn, for those who are hungry for knowledge. The following pages will lead you toward new shores of flavor and knowledge.

PENNE RIGATE WITH CREAM OF CARAMELIZED ONION AND PARMIGIANO

30 min   20 min

SERVES 4

11 oz/320 g bronze-drawn penne
    rigate or fusilli
½ cup (4¼ oz/120 g) butter
⅓ cup (2½ oz/70 g) brown sugar
12¼ oz/350 g red onion, julienned
1 bay leaf
⅓ cup (3 fl oz/90 ml) apple
    vinegar
⅔ cup (5 fl oz/150 ml) white
    vinegar
⅓ cup (2¾ fl oz/80 ml) heavy
    (double) cream
2 oz/60 g aged Parmigiano
    Reggiano, grated
thyme leaves, to garnish
salt and freshly ground black
    pepper

For the onion sauce, melt ¾ oz/20 g of the butter with the sugar in a pan over medium heat, then add the onion (setting a few slices aside for garnish) and the bay leaf and cook for 5 minutes. Add the apple vinegar and white vinegar, and a grinding of pepper, and cook until reduced almost completely, about 10 minutes.

Add the remaining butter, the cream, and the Parmigiano, stir through, then blend to a cream using an immersion blender.

Cook the pasta in plenty of salted, boiling water according to the packet instructions. Drain when al dente, transfer to the pan with the onion cream, and cook for a couple of minutes.

Before serving, garnish with a few thyme leaves and slices of onion.

PENNE RIGATE WITH TOMATO THREE WAYS AND BASIL OIL

1 hour   1 hour

SERVES 4

11 oz/320 g bronze-drawn penne
    rigate or fusilloni
10½ oz/300 g Datterino tomatoes
2¾ tablespoons extra virgin olive oil
1 tablespoon confectioners' (icing)
    sugar
1 bunch thyme
salt

FOR THE TOMATO SAUCE
2 tablespoons extra virgin olive oil
1¾ oz/50 g soffritto mix (finely
    diced celery stalk, carrot, and
    onion)
7 oz/200 g canned peeled
    tomatoes
pinch of granulated sugar

FOR THE OIL-POACHED CHERRY
    TOMATOES
⅓ cup plus 1 tablespoon (3½ fl
    oz/100 ml) extra virgin olive oil
12 cherry tomatoes, blanched for
    1 minute, cooled, and peeled
1 clove garlic, cut into thin strips

FOR THE BASIL OIL
1 bunch basil, plus extra to garnish
⅓ cup plus 1 tablespoon (3½ fl
    oz/100 ml) extra virgin olive oil

Preheat the oven to 250°F (120°C/Gas Mark ½).

Halve the Datterino tomatoes through the stem and place
on a lined sheet pan (baking tray) with the oil, confectioners'
(icing) sugar, 1 teaspoon salt, and two-thirds of the thyme,
and cook in the oven for 1 hour.

For the tomato sauce, heat a drizzle of oil in a pan over
low heat and gently cook the soffritto mix for 5 minutes
until browned. Add the peeled tomatoes, a pinch of
granulated sugar, and salt and pepper to taste, and simmer
for 10 minutes. Put to one side.

For the cherry tomatoes, heat the oil in a pan to a temperature of 175°F (80°C), and cook the tomatoes for 30 minutes,
flavoring the oil with leaves from the remaining thyme,
1 clove of garlic, and a little salt.

For the basil oil, use a blender to blend the basil leaves with
the oil, then strain, and put to one side.

Cook the pasta in plenty of salted, boiling water according
to the packet instructions. Drain 2 minutes before the
cooking time indicated, and finish cooking in the pan with
the tomato sauce for a couple of minutes. Serve with the
oil-cooked cherry tomatoes and the caramelized tomatoes,
and garnish with basil leaves and the basil oil.

Tip
Oil poaching is a technique that helps maintain all the
flavors of the food, as the hot oil forms a protective film
that stops the juices from flowing out. For best results, the
cherry tomatoes must be completely submerged in the oil.

TIMBALE OF LINGUINE WITH ZUCCHINI, CARROT, TOMATOES, AND GORGONZOLA

Little timbales to bring out the child in you. Play with the molds, exercising the imagination, and combining the green, orange, and red of the vegetables, the milky white of the Gorgonzola, and the golden yellow of the linguine.

50 min   20 min

SERVES 4

8¾ oz/250 g bronze-drawn
    linguine or spaghettoni
butter, for the molds
4 sheets phyllo (filo) dough
2 tablespoons extra virgin olive oil,
    plus extra for drizzling
2 zucchini (courgettes), diced
2 carrots, diced
3½ oz/100 g Pachino tomatoes,
    halved
2 oz/60 g Gorgonzola
⅓ cup plus 1 tablespoon
    (3½ fl oz/100 ml) milk
1 oz/30 g Parmigiano Reggiano,
    grated
fresh herbs, such as thyme or
    marjoram, to garnish
salt and freshly ground black
    pepper

Grease 4 aluminum molds, 3½–4 inches (9–10 cm) in diameter, with the butter and line them with the phyllo (filo) dough.

Cook the pasta in plenty of salted, boiling water for three-quarters of the time indicated on the packet. Drain, and cool on a sheet pan (baking tray) with a drizzle of oil.

Heat the oil in a pan over medium heat and sauté the zucchini (courgettes) and carrots with salt and pepper to taste, for 4 minutes. Add the tomatoes and cook for 1 minute, then remove from the heat.

In a pan over low heat, dissolve the Gorgonzola in the milk, adding salt and pepper to taste, and put to one side.

Preheat the oven to 350°F (180°C/Gas Mark 4).

Stir the linguine through the tomato, zucchini, and carrot sauce, fill the molds, and sprinkle with the grated Parmigiano. Cook in the oven for 5 minutes.

Spread a layer of the Gorgonzola cream on the bottom of each plate and place the timbale in the center. Garnish as you wish with fresh aromatic herbs.

Tip
As an alternative to the Gorgonzola cream, you can serve the timbale with an aromatic pesto: blend ¾ oz/20 g parsley with 2 teaspoons extra virgin olive oil and a pinch of salt until you get a smooth sauce.

TORTIGLIONI WITH PARMIGIANO FONDUE AND BALSAMIC VINEGAR

Just a few drops are enough to enjoy the unmistakable sweet and sour flavor of traditional balsamic vinegar, with woody notes of the barrels that saw it age.

15 min   15 min

SERVES 4

11 oz/320 g bronze-drawn
   tortiglioni or mezzi rigatoni
1¼ cups/300 ml heavy (double)
   cream
4¼ oz/120 g Parmigiano Reggiano,
   grated
Traditional Balsamic Vinegar of
   Modena
salt and freshly ground black
   pepper

Cook the pasta in plenty of salted, boiling water according to the packet instructions.

In the meantime, simmer the cream in a pan, add the grated Parmigiano, and mix well until you have a fondue. Adjust salt and pepper to taste and keep warm off the heat.

Drain the tortiglioni when al dente, then pour into the pan with the Parmigiano fondue and stir well.

Serve with a few drops of the Traditional Balsamic Vinegar.

Tip
You can substitute the vinegar with a very light dusting of coffee powder. Don't use too much, to avoid hiding the other flavors of the dish.

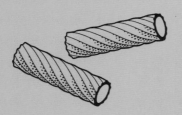

FUSILLONI WITH CREAM OF PECORINO AND POMEGRANATE

10 min   12 min

SERVES 4

11 oz/320 g bronze-drawn fusilloni
    or penne rigate
3½ tablespoons extra virgin olive
    oil
7 oz/200 g Pecorino Romano,
    grated
seeds of 1 pomegranate
salt and freshly ground black
    pepper

Cook the pasta in salted, boiling water according to the packet instructions.

In the meantime, mix the extra virgin olive oil in a bowl with the Pecorino. Dilute with a little of the pasta cooking water, add salt, if necessary, and pepper and mix well.

Drain the pasta when al dente, combine with the cream sauce, and garnish with the pomegranate seeds.

Tip
The pomegranate seeds give the dish that perfect balance of sweet and savory. For a crunchier note, you can garnish with some coarsely chopped walnuts.

FUSILLONI WITH SMOKED BUTTER, PARMIGIANO, AND SICHUAN PEPPER

20 min   11 min

SERVES 4

11 oz/320 g bronze-drawn fusilloni
   or mezzi rigatoni
½ cup (4¼ oz/120 g) smoked
   butter
3½ oz/100 g aged Parmigiano
   Reggiano, grated
20 Sichuan peppercorns
salt

Cook the pasta in plenty of salted, boiling water according to the packet instructions.

In the meantime, in a mixing bowl, beat the smoked butter with half of the Parmigiano until you have a smooth cream.

Lightly toast the peppercorns in a pan, then grind them well with a meat tenderizer or a pestle and mortar.

Drain the pasta when al dente, reserving a little of the pasta cooking water. Mix the pasta with the butter in the mixing bowl, adding a few spoonfuls of the cooking water, if needed, for a smooth sauce.

Divide the pasta between 4 bowls and garnish with the ground Sichuan pepper and the remaining Parmigiano.

Tip
You can smoke the butter while cold using a smoker oven, to lend it the perfect flavor of dried rosemary (1 well-dried sprig is enough). Alternatively, you can buy the butter already smoked.

FUSILLONI WITH ZUCCHINI, CHERRY TOMATOES, AND RICOTTA SALATA

15 min   15 min

SERVES 4

11 oz/320 g bronze-drawn fusilloni
    or fusilli
4 tablespoons extra virgin olive oil
¾ oz/20 g leek, julienned
10½ oz/300 g zucchini
    (courgettes), diced
1¾ oz/50 g cherry tomatoes,
    quartered
10 basil leaves
⅛ cup (1 oz/30 g) grated ricotta
    salata
salt and freshly ground black
    pepper

In a preheated pan, add 2 tablespoons of oil and the leek, and cook for 3–4 minutes. Once softened, add the zucchini (courgettes) and salt and pepper to taste, then cook quickly, for 2 minutes, so the vegetables remain crunchy.

To the same pan, add the remaining oil and quickly fry the cherry tomatoes.

Cook the pasta in plenty of salted, boiling water according to the packet instructions. Drain when al dente and sauté briefly in the pan with the vegetables.

Divide the pasta between 4 plates, and garnish with ripped basil leaves and slivers of ricotta salata before serving.

RICOTTA

Fresh ricotta is a dairy product with a delicate, creamy texture that is often used in the preparation of desserts as well as savory dishes. Obtained from whey, it has a slightly sweet flavor and lactic note. Thanks to its creaminess, it is excellent for use in pasta sauces, particularly when paired with black pepper, the zest of citrus fruits, or seasonal vegetables.

Ricotta salata, despite sharing a common base with the fresh version, differs notably in its production process and consistency, undergoing a longer drying and salting period. It is pressed and left to mature for several weeks or months, giving it its savory, slightly spicy flavor.

In Italian gastronomic tradition, ricotta salata is served as an appetizer, and in fresh salads, risottos, and pasta dishes, creating interesting contrasts thanks to its strong taste.

FUSILLONI WITH PEPPERS AND LEEKS

15 min   20 min

SERVES 4

11 oz/320 g bronze-drawn fusilloni
    or fusilli
4 tablespoons extra virgin olive oil
2¾ oz/80 g soft bread (no crust),
    crumbled
1 clove garlic, peeled and halved
handful of fresh herbs, such as
    thyme or basil, finely chopped
8¾ oz/250 g red bell pepper,
    deseeded and diced
3½ oz/100 g leeks, julienned
2 small potatoes, diced
1 oz/25 g oil-packed anchovy
    fillets
salt and freshly ground black
    pepper

Heat 1 tablespoon of oil in a pan and toast the bread with ½ clove of garlic until browned. Leave to cool slightly, then discard the garlic and add the chopped fresh herbs. Put to one side.

Heat another tablespoon of oil in the same pan and sauté the bell pepper for 3 minutes. Put to one side.

In a separate pan, heat the remaining oil and the remaining ½ clove of garlic for 1–2 minutes, then add the leeks and cook until browned, about 5 minutes. Add the potatoes and enough water to cover, and bring to a boil for 10 minutes.

Add the anchovies and salt and pepper to taste, and blend using an immersion blender. You should get a flavorsome, rather liquid mixture. Put to one side.

In the meantime, cook the pasta in plenty of salted, boiling water according to the packet instructions. Drain when al dente, add to the pan with the peppers, and sauté for 2 minutes.

Serve the pasta with the bell pepper on a layer of the leek and anchovy sauce, sprinkled with the crunchy, herb-scented bread.

MACCHEROTTI WITH CREAM OF ASPARAGUS

30 min   15 min

SERVES 4

11 oz/320 g bronze-drawn
   maccherotti or mezzi rigatoni
14 oz/400 g asparagus, cut into
   rounds (tips set aside)
2 tablespoons extra virgin olive oil
1 shallot, chopped
½ clove garlic
a few mint leaves
a few basil leaves
salt and freshly ground black
   pepper

Blanch the asparagus in salted, boiling water for 2–3 minutes, then quickly transfer to a bowl of iced water. Keep ⅓ cup (3 fl of/80 ml) of the cooking water to one side.

Heat the oil in a pan over medium heat and cook the chopped shallot and garlic clove for 2–3 minutes. When browned, add the blanched asparagus, adding salt and pepper to taste, then flavor with the ripped mint and basil leaves. Pour the reserved cooking water into the pan and leave to cook for 10 minutes, then blend everything in a blender.

In the meantime, cook the pasta in plenty of salted, boiling water according to the packet instructions. Drain when al dente, then sauté in a pan with the cream of asparagus and the asparagus tips for a couple of minutes.

SPAGHETTONI WITH MUSSELS, SQUID, AND SHRIMP EN PAPILLOTE

The scent of shrimp (prawns), mussels, and squid evokes an image of fishing boats moored in the port in the early morning. A simple base of fried garlic and parsley, the final touch of the tomato sauce, and the sea is ready to be served.

30 min   18 min

SERVES 4

11 oz/320 g bronze-drawn
    spaghettoni or linguine
3 tablespoons plus 1½ teaspoons
    extra virgin olive oil
1 clove garlic, crushed
7 oz/200 g mussels, cleaned
    (see page 70)
1 tablespoon chopped parsley
7 oz/200 g squid, cleaned (see
    page 60) and cut into slices
7 oz/200 g tomato sauce
    (passata)
3½ oz/100 g shrimp (prawn) tails
salt and freshly ground black
    pepper

Heat the oil in a pan over medium heat, add the garlic, and cook for 30 seconds. Once browned, add the mussels and the chopped parsley. Cover, and cook until all the mussels are open, 3–4 minutes. Add the squid and the tomato sauce, then finally the shrimp (prawn) tails, and leave to cook for 10 minutes. Add salt and pepper to taste.

Prepare some baking parchment for the papillote on a sheet pan (baking tray) and preheat the oven to 400°F (200°C/Gas Mark 6).

In the meantime, cook the pasta in plenty of salted, boiling water according to the packet instructions. Remove from the heat 2 minutes earlier than the time indicated, drain, and add to the seafood sauce, mixing it well in the pan. Pour it all onto the baking parchment and close the parcel, sealing the edges.

Cook in the oven for 3 minutes, after which you should open the papillote carefully and return to the oven for a further 2 minutes.

Tip
Add more color and flavor to the dish by stirring 1 sachet of saffron dissolved in a little hot water into the sauce.

LINGUINE WITH LOBSTER AND CHERRY TOMATOES

Its pink-white meat and decisive flavor make lobster a much-esteemed crustacean. This recipe is perfect for holiday lunches or to transform a normal Sunday meal into a masterpiece.

20 min   20 min

SERVES 4

11 oz/320 g bronze-drawn linguine
   or mezzi rigatoni
2 tablespoons extra virgin olive oil
½ small onion, chopped
2 lobsters, 8¾ oz/250 g each, cut
   in half lengthwise
⅓ cup plus 1 tablespoon (3½ fl
   oz/100 ml) white wine
14 oz/400 g cherry tomatoes,
   halved
¾ oz/20 g parsley, chopped
¾ oz/20 g oregano leaves
salt and freshly ground black
   pepper

Heat the oil in a wide pan over medium heat and add the onion. Cook for 5 minutes and, once browned, increase the heat and add the lobsters. Leave to brown for 1 minute, then add the wine and leave to evaporate, 3–4 minutes, then turn down the heat and add salt and pepper to taste. Add the tomatoes and cook for a further 8–10 minutes until the tomatoes have broken down.

Remove the lobster meat from the shells and cut into large pieces, then return to the sauce. Discard the shells.

In the meantime, cook the pasta in plenty of salted, boiling water according to the packet instructions. Drain when al dente, and serve the pasta with the sauce prepared earlier, the parsley, and oregano.

Tip
Give a crunchy touch to the final dish with 2 tablespoons of toasted pine nuts or slivered almonds.

LINGUINE WITH SHRIMP AND PISTACHIO PESTO

15 min   12 min

SERVES 4

11 oz/320 g bronze-drawn linguine
    or spaghettoni
1 cup (5¼ oz/150 g) pistachios,
    shelled
¼ cup (1 oz/30 g) pine nuts
¼ cup (1 oz/30 g) blanched
    almonds
⅓ cup (1 oz/30 g) walnut kernels
1 clove garlic, coarsely chopped
5 mint leaves
2 oz/60 g Parmigiano Reggiano,
    grated
⅓ cup plus 1 tablespoon (3½ fl
    oz/100 ml) extra virgin olive oil,
    plus extra to drizzle
8 jumbo shrimp (king prawns),
    cleaned and shelled
salt and freshly ground black
    pepper

Put the pistachios in a blender (set some aside to garnish the dish) with the pine nuts, almonds, walnuts, garlic, mint leaves, Parmigiano, and three-quarters of the oil. Blend everything together, and when you have a smooth mixture, adjust the seasoning with a pinch of salt and a dusting of pepper.

Cook the pasta in plenty of salted, boiling water according to the packet instructions.

In the meantime, fry the shrimp in a pan on medium-high heat with a drizzle of oil and salt and pepper to taste for 2–3 minutes until the flesh is pink.

Drain the linguine when al dente, retaining a little of the cooking water. Add the pasta to the pan with the king prawns and, off the heat, add the pesto and mix well, adding some of the cooking water, if necessary. Garnish with the reserved pistachios.

LINGUINE WITH GARLIC, OIL, CHILI PEPPER, BOTTARGA, AND LEMON

20 min   15 min

SERVES 4

11 oz/320 g bronze-drawn linguine
   or spaghettoni
⅓ cup (3 fl oz/80 ml) extra virgin
   olive oil
1 fresh red chili pepper, finely
   chopped
2 cloves garlic, peeled and whole
grated zest of ½ unwaxed lemon
1½ oz/40 g mullet bottarga, thinly
   sliced
salt

Gently heat two-thirds of the oil in a pan on medium heat. Add the chili pepper and cook for 1–2 minutes, then put to one side.

Blanch the garlic cloves for 1 minute in boiling water, then plunge into cold water. Repeat the blanching and chilling another four times. Then put the garlic in a blender with a little of the remaining oil and blend until you get a smooth, fragrant cream.

Cook the pasta in plenty of salted, boiling water for two-thirds of the cooking time indicated on the packet. Drain, and finish cooking in the pan with the previously prepared oil for 2 minutes. Add the garlic cream and mix well.

Divide among 4 plates and sprinkle with the lemon zest and bottarga before serving.

Tip
The bottarga and lemon zest lend the dish salty and decisive fish tones and citrus freshness respectively, both in perfect union with the linguine. If you wish, you can substitute the lemon with orange zest.

LINGUINE WITH LANGOUSTINE, MARJORAM, AND BOTTARGA

The fresh, penetrating aroma of the marjoram blends with the complex character of the bottarga, while the langoustine, a delicacy of the sea, and linguine are ready to soak up that sauce. Keep those napkins at hand!

20 min   11 min

SERVES 4

11 oz/320 g bronze-drawn linguine or mezzi rigatoni

2¾ tablespoons extra virgin olive oil

16 langoustine tails

1 small bunch marjoram: 1 sprig set aside, the rest chopped

⅓ cup plus 1 tablespoon (3½ fl oz/100 ml) cooking (single) cream

7 oz/200 g cherry tomatoes, halved

1 oz/30 g mullet bottarga, grated

salt and freshly ground black pepper

Heat half of the oil in a pan on medium heat, and sauté the langoustine tails for 3–4 minutes until cooked through. Put the tails to one side.

In the same pan, warm the chopped marjoram for a few minutes in the rest of the oil. Add salt and pepper to taste, then add the cream and tomatoes and continue cooking for 5 minutes. After 4 minutes, put the langoustine tails back in to the pan to warm for the final minute.

Cook the pasta in plenty of salted, boiling water according to the packet instructions. Drain when al dente, then add to the sauce and cook for 2 minutes. Garnish the pasta with the bottarga and the remaining marjoram leaves before serving.

Tip

If you prefer, you can substitute the cream with 3½ oz/100 g cherry tomatoes, which will give the same creaminess.

LINGUINE WITH SEAFOOD AND CRUNCHY VEGETABLES EN PAPILLOTE

As you dive into the glossy bronze-drawn linguine, it's a celebration of the sea. And an idea of happiness that flows in through the windows on a breeze.

40 min   20 min

SERVES 4

11 oz/320 g bronze-drawn linguine
   or spaghettoni
2¾ tablespoons extra virgin olive
   oil, plus extra for frying and
   drizzling
3 cloves garlic
parsley, stalks and leaves
10½ oz/300 g mussels, cleaned
   (see page 70)
10½ oz/300 g cross-cut carpet
   shell clams, cleaned (see page
   57)
1¾ oz/50 g zucchini (courgette),
   julienned
1¾ oz/50 g carrot, julienned
1 oz/30 g celery stalk, julienned
1½ oz/40 eggplant (aubergine),
   julienned
3½ oz/100 g cherry tomatoes,
   halved
2¾ oz/80 g shrimp (prawn) tails
3½ oz/100 g squid, cleaned (see
   page 60) and cut into strips
5¼ oz/150 g fillet of rockfish, diced
3½ oz/100 g musky octopus,
   cleaned and cut into strips
1 sprig basil
chili powder, to taste
salt

Heat the oil in a pan with the garlic and parsley stalks, then cook the mussels and clams until they open, 3–4 minutes. When completely opened, strain the cooking liquid into a bowl, remove and discard some of the shells, then place the shellfish in a bowl with the cooking water.

Heat a drizzle of oil in a nonstick pan and sauté the zucchini (courgette), carrot, celery, and eggplant (aubergine) for 2 minutes.

Quickly sautè each single fish in a pan with 2 tablespoons of oil.

Heat another drizzle of oil in a pan and sauté the tomatoes for 2 minutes, adding salt to taste (the tomatoes should become deeper in color, but remain intact).

Cook the pasta in plenty of salted, boiling water for half of the time instructed on the packet. Place all of the ingredients prepared previously in a large pan, adding some of the mollusk broth. Drain the pasta, then cook it briefly in the sauce, mixing well. Adjust salt and chili pepper to taste.

Preheat the oven to 350°F (180°C/Gas Mark 4).

Take 4 sheets of baking parchment and divide the linguine among them with a drizzle of oil. Complete with a few leaves of chopped basil and parsley and close the papers, sealing the edges. Place in the oven for around 10 minutes until cooked through.

Tip
You can substitute the rockfish with the same quantity of seabass fillets, and the musky octopus with the same quantity of octopus, precooked and vacuum-packed.

BRONZE DRAWING: AN ANCIENT STORY

"Maccheroni made with a fine dough, worked over a long time, greatly compressed, and passed through special molds, come in various qualities and can be found everywhere at a modest price." So wrote the German poet Goethe in his famous *Italian Journey* (1787), describing the maccheronari (sellers) he passed on the street corners of Naples, their pasta wrapped in pieces of paper, making "incredible sales." The "special molds" Goethe describes are dies.

A die is a metal plate with a number of holes of different shapes and sizes, which create the final design or shape of the pasta. During the extrusion ("drawing") process, the mixture of semolina and water is compressed through the holes of the die, which gives the pasta its shape. Drawing is a crucial step for the pasta maker, whose art lies in knowing how to prepare the correct dough for each die, starting with the texture of the mixture of water and semolina, and calculating the humidity and resistance.

Is it possible to reconstruct the birth of the die? In medieval Italy, "dry" pasta shapes (so-called to differentiate them from various broths) were essentially obtained in one of two ways: dragging or cutting. Even now, trofie and orecchiette are formed through dragging.

In the eleventh century, goldsmiths and smiths of other precious metals developed tools to produce increasingly long metal threads just a few millimetres thick, and so the technique of micro-drawing through extrusion was born. There is no historical certainty, but it is possible that the pasta makers copied the goldsmiths' use of molds, or dies, to draw their pasta mixture through.

Written testimony of this "maccheroni device"—the torque for making pasta—comes from Cristoforo da Messisbugo, chef at the court of Ferrara in the first half of the sixteenth century and author of culinary treatises. The Neapolitan pasta makers were the first to adopt this device between the sixteenth and seventeenth centuries, as reported in several historical documents.

Towards the end of the eighteenth century, the first technical descriptions of the device appear, for example that found in the *Arts du Vermicelier* (1767) by French doctor and chemist Paul-Jacques Malouin, who described in detail the process of making vermicelli both in France and Italy. Between the end of the nineteenth century and the beginning of the twentieth, the advent of steam engines and then that of electricity changed the methods of processing pasta, and the metal torques became increasingly efficient.

Today, there are over three hundred different pasta shapes.

Bronze drawing is now one of the best-known and recognized pasta-making processes in Italy. The inserts of the dies are products of high-precision mechanical engineering—interchangeable and easily replaced when worn. Thanks to their high-friction coefficient, bronze inserts are able to "scratch" the pasta as it comes out, resulting in a rough final surface and increasing its ability to hold onto sauces.

FUSILLI WITH RED SHRIMP, MANGO, AND RASPBERRIES

1 hour   25 min

SERVES 4

11 oz/320 g bronze-drawn fusilli or
  mezzi rigatoni
12 red shrimp (prawns)
4 tablespoons extra virgin olive oil
1 oz/25 g leeks, very finely diced
1 oz/25 g shallots, very finely diced
1 bay leaf
1 tablespoon Cognac
3 tablespoons plus 1½ teaspoons
  white wine
1 teaspoon tomato paste (purée)
3 cups (1½ pints/700 ml) cold
  water
⅝ cup (5 oz/150 g) boiled rice
3½ oz/100 g Pecorino Romano,
  grated
¾ cups (½ pint/200 ml) lukewarm
  water
¾ cup (3½ oz/100 g) raspberries
1 fresh mango, not too ripe, flesh
  diced
grated zest of 1 lime
1 tablespoon finely chopped
  thyme
1 tablespoon finely chopped
  marjoram
salt and freshly ground black
  pepper

Clean and shell the shrimp (prawns), keeping the heads and shells.

Prepare the bisque by heating 2 tablespoons of oil in a pan over medium heat, and cooking the leeks, shallots, and bay leaf for 2–3 minutes until softened. Add the shrimp (prawn) heads and shells, crush them, and toast them over high heat for 1 minute, then add the Cognac and allow to flambée.

Add the white wine to the pan, scraping the base of the pan to deglaze, and cook until the wine has evaporated and the sauce reduced, 3–4 minutes. Add the tomato paste (purée) and cover with the cold water. Cook for around 15–20 minutes, removing any froth from the surface with a skimmer.

Strain through a fine chinois into a clean pan, discarding the solids. Add the rice, boil for a couple of minutes, then blend to a thick cream, the same consistency as mayonnaise, and add salt to taste. Transfer to a piping bag and leave to cool.

Cut the shrimp into pieces and toss with the remaining oil. Cover and leave in the fridge.

Blend the Pecorino with the lukewarm water until you have a uniform cream, adding some freshly ground black pepper.

Cook the pasta in plenty of salted, boiling water for 10 minutes, then drain when al dente and retain the cooking water. In a bowl, mix the pasta with the Pecorino cream, stirring quickly and adding a little of the cooking water if necessary. Add the shrimp and serve, completing the dish with the raspberries and mango. Garnish with a drizzle of the bisque and the lime zest, thyme, marjoram, and pepper.

MEZZI RIGATONI WITH LOBSTER, CONFIT TOMATOES, AND ZUCCHINI

1 hour   1 hour

SERVES 4

11 oz/320 g bronze-drawn mezzi
    rigatoni or linguine
1 lobster (around 21 oz/600 g)
2 oz/60 g soffritto mix (finely
    diced celery stalk, carrot, and
    onion)
1 fresh red chili pepper, chopped
1 bunch of fresh herbs (sage,
    rosemary, thyme, parsley, or
    basil), plus extra sprigs of
    thyme and parsley
7 oz/200 g Datterino tomatoes
3 tablespoons brown sugar
2¾ tablespoons extra virgin olive
    oil, plus extra for drizzling
1 clove garlic, peeled and halved
7 oz/200 g zucchini (courgettes),
    cubed
¼ cup (1 oz/30 g) toasted pine
    nuts, to garnish
salt

Preheat the oven to 210°F (100°C/Gas Mark ¼). Cut the lobster in half lengthwise and remove the meat from the shells, reserving the shells. Cut the meat into small cubes.

Put the soffritto mix, chili pepper, and the bunch of herbs in a saucepan, add the lobster shells, and brown well over medium heat for 5 minutes. Add 2 cups (17fl oz/500 ml) of water and start cooking until you get a *fumet* (reduction) that you will need for cooking the mezzi rigatoni.

Place the tomatoes on a sheet pan (baking tray), add the sugar, a drizzle of oil, sprigs of thyme, and salt to taste, and cook in the oven for 1 hour.

Put the oil, half a garlic clove, and a parsley sprig in a hot pan, brown for a few moments, add the lobster meat and a little salt. Once cooked, 6–7 minutes, set the lobster aside.

In the same pan, cook the zucchini (courgettes), the remaining half garlic clove, and another parsley sprig. After around 5 minutes, add the cooked lobster and mix well.

Cook the pasta in plenty of salted, boiling water for half the time suggested on the packet. Drain the pasta, then return to the pan and add the lobster and zucchini sauce, then gradually add the lobster *fumet* until the pasta has finished cooking. Just before the end of the cooking time, stir through the caramelized tomatoes.

Before serving, garnish with finely chopped parsley and pine nuts.

MEZZI RIGATONI WITH WHITE BUTTER, RED SHRIMP, AND CAPER DUST

The suave acidity of the white butter (a sauce from northern Italy for fish and crustaceans) becomes the binding agent between the pasta and shrimp (prawn) meat, whose sweetness is mirrored in the brininess of the toasted capers.

30 min   50 min

SERVES 4

11 oz/320 g bronze-drawn mezzi rigatoni or linguine
2 shallots, peeled and whole
⅓ cup plus 1 tablespoon (3½ fl oz/100 ml) white wine
⅓ cup plus 1 tablespoon (3½ fl oz/100 ml) white vinegar
scant ½ cup (3½ oz/100 g) butter, cold
12 red shrimp (prawn) tails
3 tablespoons extra virgin olive oil
grated zest of 1 lemon
3 tablespoons salt-packed Pantelleria capers
marjoram leaves, to garnish
salt

For the white butter, put the shallots, wine, and vinegar into a pan and heat until reduced by about half. Discard the shallots and whisk the cold butter into the reduced liquid.

Cut the shrimp (prawn) tails into a coarse tartare, and garnish with the oil, a little salt, and lemon zest.

For the caper dust, dehydrate the capers on a sheet pan (baking tray) lined with baking parchment in a conventional oven at 100°F/40°C/Gas Mark ¼ (or in a desiccator) for around 50 minutes, then whizz to dust in a blender.

In the meantime, cook the pasta in plenty of salted, boiling water according to the packet instructions. Drain when al dente, and stir through the white butter and some of the shrimp tartare. Serve, and complete each plate with the remaining shrimp tartare, a few marjoram leaves, and the caper dust.

Tip
The caper dust is the ideal seasoning for fish and vegetable dishes. For a quicker preparation of this recipe, you can complete the dish with a handful of capers rinsed of salt.

MEZZI RIGATONI WITH TUNA, BOTTARGA, AND WILD FENNEL

A Mediterranean dream of bottarga, tuna, and wild fennel gathered in uncultivated fields or near dry stone walls in the sun. Finally, the mezzi rigatoni, with their cylinder shape and ribbed texture, collect and elevate the sauce.

25 min   14 min

SERVES 4

11 oz/320 g bronze-drawn mezzi rigatoni or conchiglie rigate
2 tablespoons extra virgin olive oil
4¼ oz/120 g onion, finely sliced
7 oz/200 g fresh tuna, diced
1 tablespoon plus 1½ teaspoons capers
⅓ cup plus 1 tablespoon (3½ fl oz/100 ml) white wine
⅓ cup plus 1 tablespoon (3½ fl oz/100 ml) fish broth (stock) (optional)
3½ oz/100 g tomatoes, cut into pieces
1 oz/30 g wild fennel, chopped
¾ oz/20 g mullet bottarga, grated
salt and freshly ground black pepper

Heat the oil in a pan over medium heat and cook the onion for 5 minutes. Add the tuna, cook for 2 minutes, then add the capers. Add the white wine, and leave to simmer and evaporate for 3–4 minutes, adding salt and pepper to taste.

If necessary, moisten the tuna with the fish broth, then add the tomatoes and half of the wild fennel. If the sauce is too dry, add a little more fish broth.

Cook the pasta in plenty of salted, boiling water according to the packet instructions. Drain when al dente, and garnish with the sauce. Add the remaining wild fennel and sprinkle over the bottarga.

Tip
You can substitute the tuna with the same quantity of amberjack or sea bass fillets. For a more delicate dish, substitute the bottarga with 4 tablespoons of bread crumbs sautéed in a nonstick pan with a drizzle of extra virgin olive oil scented with fresh thyme.

BOTTARGA

From the Arabic term *buṭārikh*, bottarga is obtained via a process of salting and drying the roe pouch of either grey mullet or tuna. Once extracted, the fish eggs are salted and pressed, creating a compact mass which is then dried. The result is a solid block, usually amber or orange in color, and rich in the aroma and flavor of the sea, making it a very popular ingredient due to its strong character.

In Italy, two of the main centers of production of mullet bottarga in particular are Cabras in Sardinia, and Orbetello in Tuscany. Mullet bottarga is intense and salty on the palate. It is mainly used grated over pasta, and is excellent paired with citrus peel, which lends it an extra freshness. Thinly sliced, drizzled with oil, and accompanied by slices of crusty bread, it also makes a unique appetizer. Much appreciated in Mediterranean cuisine, mullet bottarga gives dishes a touch of elegance and authenticity, recalling ancient mari-time traditions and a taste of the sea.

MACCHEROTTI WITH SEAFOOD CARBONARA

That is the way of the ocean: sometimes calm, other times agitated, yet always able to provide us with sumptuous delights. Here is a recipe for you to lose yourself in a sea of flavor.

2 hours   50 min

SERVES 4

11 oz/320 g bronze-drawn maccherotti or mezzi rigatoni
extra virgin olive oil
3½ oz/100 g each clams and mussels, cleaned (see pages 57 and 70)
1 oz/30 g salmon roe
1 oz/30 g tuna bottarga
1¼ oz/50 g sea urchin roe
¾ oz/20 g scallop roe
1 shallot, finely chopped
1 clove garlic, sliced
1 fresh red chili pepper, chopped
⅓ cup (3 fl oz/80 ml) white wine
2 cups (17 fl oz/500 ml) fish broth (stock)
grated zest of 1 lime
¾ oz/18 g caviar (we use Osetra)
salt and white pepper

FOR THE SHRIMP BROTH
6 red jumbo shrimp
1 shallot, coarsely chopped
1 celery stalk, coarsely chopped
2 cloves garlic, coarsely chopped

FOR THE SEAFOOD CARBONARA
5¼ oz/150 g guanciale (pork cheek lard), cut into strips
3½ oz/100 g amberjack fillets
2 small scallops

Heat 3 tablespoons of oil in a pan and cook the mussels and clams until they open, 3–4 minutes. Remove and discard the shells. In a blender, blend the shellfish with the salmon roe, bottarga, sea urchin roe, and scallop roe until you get a fine mixture. Transfer to the fridge.

For the shrimp (prawn) broth, separate the meat of the shrimp from the heads and shells. In a small pan, toast the heads and shells in 1 tablespoon oil. Add the vegetables, toast for 3 minutes, then cover with ice. Add 2 cups (17 fl oz/500 ml) water and leave to simmer on low heat, adjusting salt and pepper to taste. After 10 minutes, discard the impurities floating to the surface of the water. Leave to simmer for a further 10 minutes. Strain the broth and put to one side.

For the seafood carbonara, put the guanciale in a pan over low heat to render the fat. Strain off the fat and put to one side. Cut the amberjack into small pieces. Clean the scallops and discard the coral, then season the amberjack and scallops with salt and pepper. In a pan, bring the strained fat to 110°F/44°C and slowly cook the amberjack and scallops at that temperature for 15 minutes. Once cooked, lay them on some paper towels and transfer to the oven at 115°F/45°C/Gas Mark ¼ to keep warm.

Heat 4 tablespoons of oil in a pan and brown the shallot, garlic, and chili pepper for 2–3 minutes. Add the wine and cook for 3–4 minutes. Add ⅓ cup plus 1 tablespoon (3½ fl oz/100 ml) each of the shrimp and fish broths.

Cook the pasta in plenty of salted, boiling water for 6 minutes, then drain and pour into the pan with the sauce. Stir, add the fish and shrimp broths, and cook for 3 minutes—the pasta must be very al dente. Once cooked, stir through the blended shellfish and roe and a sprinkling of lime zest.

Season the shrimp meat, then chop into small pieces. Complete the dish with a quenelle of shrimp and caviar. Add the amberjack and scallops, and serve.

MACCHEROTTI WITH LANGOUSTINES AND CHERRY TOMATOES

The freshness of the langoustines unites with the maccherotti in this light, elegant recipe that is ideal for a summer lunch on the terrace or dinner among friends.

20 min   10 min

SERVES 4

11 oz/320 g bronze-drawn maccherotti or penne rigate
6 tablespoons extra virgin olive oil
1 clove garlic, peeled and whole
1 dried chili pepper
12 langoustines, cut in half lengthwise
7 oz/200 g cherry tomatoes, cut into quarters
2 tablespoons white wine
1 oz/30 g parsley, finely chopped
salt

Heat half of the oil in a pan over medium heat with the whole garlic clove for 1–2 minutes. When it starts to brown, add the chili pepper and the langoustines and cook for 2 minutes. Add the white wine and leave to simmer and evaporate, then add the tomatoes. Leave to cook for 5 minutes, add salt to taste, and stir through the parsley. Remove and discard the garlic clove and chili pepper.

In the meantime, cook the pasta in plenty of salted, boiling water according to the packet instructions. Drain when al dente, retaining some of the pasta cooking water, and stir into the pan with the langoustine sauce. Add a little of the pasta cooking water if needed, and the remaining oil.

Tip
You can substitute the langoustines with other crustaceans, such as shrimp (prawns) or different varieties of lobster.

MEZZE PENNE WITH SALMON, YOGURT, AND PARSLEY PESTO

30 min   12 min

SERVES 4

11 oz/320 g bronze-drawn mezze
    penne or penne rigate
3½ tablespoons (1¾ oz/50 g)
    butter
2 tablespoons extra virgin olive oil
1 sprig dill, plus extra to serve
5 oz/140 g smoked salmon, cut
    into strips
⅔ cup (5¼ oz/150 g) plain yogurt
1 tablespoon smoked paprika
salt and freshly ground black
    pepper

FOR THE PARSLEY PESTO
1¾ oz/50 g parsley
1 oz/30 g day-old bread, diced
1 tablespoon white wine vinegar
¼ clove garlic
3 tablespoons plus 1½ teaspoons
    extra virgin olive oil

For the pesto, blend together the parsley, bread, vinegar, garlic, and oil until you get a parsley pesto; add salt and pepper to taste, and cover with plastic wrap (cling film).

In a pan, sauté the butter, oil, and dill with 3½ oz/100 g smoked salmon for 1 minute. Leave to cool, then add the yogurt.

Cook the pasta in plenty of salted, boiling water according to the packet instructions. Drain when al dente, and stir through the sauce off the heat for 1 minute.

Spread a layer of the parsley pesto on each plate, lay the pasta on top, and complete with a little more smoked salmon, a light dusting of paprika, and some dill leaves.

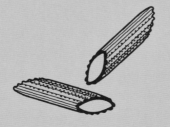

PENNE RIGATE WITH RED MULLET, SEA URCHIN, AND CUTTLEFISH INK

It is no surprise that cuttlefish use their ink to defend themselves from the predators of the ocean depths; nor that the intense flavor of the sea infuses these dishes. What is surprising are the amazing chromatic effects that the cuttlefish ink creates.

1 hour   30 min

SERVES 4

11 oz/320 g bronze-drawn penne rigate or linguine

14 oz/400 g red mullet, scaled, filleted, and deboned (reserve all bones for the *fumet*)

extra virgin olive oil, for marinating, cooking, and serving

grated zest and juice of 1 unwaxed lemon

3½ oz/100 g soffritto mix (finely diced celery stalk, carrot, and onion)

sprigs of thyme

⅓ cup (2¾ fl oz/80 ml) white wine

1 lb/500 g Datterino tomatoes, halved

1 x 4 g sachet cuttlefish ink

¾ oz/20 g sea urchin pulp

salt and white pepper

Fillet the red mullet, setting to one side the bones and heads for the *fumet*. Wash the fillets carefully in a sieve or colander under running water.

Divide the fillets in half lengthwise. Put the belly to one side, then cut the rest into strips and leave to marinate with a little oil, salt, white pepper, 1 tablespoon lemon juice, and some lemon zest. Cover with plastic wrap (cling film) and leave at room temperature for half an hour.

Heat a drizzle of oil in a small pan and brown the soffritto mix with a few sprigs of thyme. Add the mullet bones and heads, brown well, then add the white wine and cook until it evaporates, about 5 minutes. Cook for another 10 minutes over medium heat, then strain the *fumet* through a sieve into a bowl.

Heat a little oil in a pan and cook the chopped fish belly for 2–3 minutes. Add the tomatoes and adjust salt and pepper to taste. Leave the tomatoes to cook until lightly browned, then add the *fumet* and simmer for 2–3 minutes.

In the meantime, cook the pasta in plenty of salted, boiling water according to the packet instructions. Drain while still very al dente and pour into the sauce. Mix well, adding oil until you get a smooth cream, and pepper to taste.

Complete the dish with the sea urchin pulp and the marinated red mullet strips. Garnish with lemon zest and add a few drops of cuttlefish ink and oil.

Tip
You can substitute the cuttlefish ink with a little grated mullet bottarga sprinkled over the plates before serving.

PENNE RIGATE WITH SWORDFISH AND ZUCCHINI

The fried zucchini (courgettes) and ricotta salata give this swordfish sauce a strong and unusual character.

20 min   15 min

SERVES 4

11 oz/320 g bronze-drawn penne rigate or mezzi rigatoni
10½ oz/300 g zucchini (courgettes), diced
all-purpose (plain) flour, for dusting
vegetable oil, for frying
⅓ cup (3 fl oz/80 ml) extra virgin olive oil
1 clove garlic, finely chopped
7 oz/200 g swordfish, diced
¾ cup (5¾ fl oz/170ml) white wine
8¾ oz/250 g cherry tomatoes, cut into wedges
¼ oz/10 g basil leaves
⅖ cup (3½ oz/100 g) ricotta salata
salt and freshly ground black pepper

Dust the zucchini (courgette) cubes in flour, and fry in plenty of hot vegetable oil in a skillet (frying pan) for 3 minutes until golden in color. Drain, and dry on paper towels, then set to one side to cool.

Heat the extra virgin olive oil in a pan over medium heat with the garlic for 1–2 minutes, then add the swordfish and salt to taste. Increase the heat to high, add the white wine, and cook until evaporated.

Add the cherry tomatoes and some black pepper, then reduce the heat to low, and simmer for a few minutes. Add the fried zucchini and ripped basil leaves, and leave to cook for 2 minutes.

Cook the pasta in plenty of salted, boiling water according to the packet instructions. Drain when al dente, and stir through the sauce. Serve with the ricotta salata.

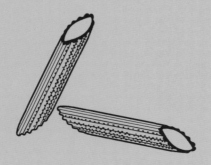

PENNE RIGATE WITH LOBSTER AND ZUCCHINI

1 hour 30 min

SERVES 4

11 oz/320 g bronze-drawn penne
   rigate or linguine
6 tablespoons extra virgin olive oil
½ small onion, chopped
2 lobsters, 8¾ oz/250 g each, cut
   in half lengthwise
⅓ cup plus 1 tablespoon (3½ fl
   oz/100 ml) white wine
14 oz/400 g cherry tomatoes,
   halved
1 clove garlic, chopped
7 oz/200 g zucchini (courgettes),
   diced
¾ cup (¾ oz/20 g) chopped parsley
salt and freshly ground black
   pepper

Heat 4 tablespoons of oil in a wide pan over medium heat and add the onion. Cook for 3–4 minutes and, once browned, increase the heat and add the lobsters. Leave to brown for 2 minutes, then add the wine and, once it is evaporated, turn down the heat and add salt and pepper to taste. Add the tomatoes and cook for a further 6–8 minutes; the sauce shouldn't be too dry.

Brown the garlic clove in the remaining oil for a minute or two, then add the zucchini (courgettes), and cook for 5 minutes.

Remove the lobster meat from the shells and cut into large pieces. Then return to the tomato sauce with the zucchini and chopped parsley.

In the meantime, cook the pasta in plenty of salted, boiling water according to the packet instructions. Drain when al dente, garnish with the sauce, and serve.

Tip
If you prefer a stronger flavor, you can substitute the zucchini (courgettes) with the same quantity of bell peppers: cut into strips and cook according to the recipe.

ALTERNATIVE METHODS OF COOKING PASTA

One of the great things about pasta is its versatility—particularly in its cooking methods.

One alternative to traditional cooking is **oven baking**, which—generally speaking—tends to favor short pasta shapes, such as rigatoni, tortiglioni, penne, and ziti tagliati, whose hollow shape enables it to "hold" the sauce. After cooking in salted, boiling water, the pasta is drained while still very al dente, garnished with ragù or another previously prepared sauce, perhaps a generous dusting of grated cheese, then placed in a nonstick sheet pan (baking tray) and put in the oven at 350°F (180°C/Gas Mark 4) for 15–20 minutes. Oven baking gives the pasta a crunchy texture on the outside, while the center—if the sauce is perfectly measured—stays soft. Don't worry if the pasta isn't perfectly al dente after baking; this type of preparation allows for a slight overcooking of the pasta, a nostalgic memory of the many times that Italian nonnas—with so much on their minds—left the tray of pasta in the oven a little too long.

Foil cooking also requires partial traditional cooking of the pasta—in this case, spaghetti or another long pasta—which is then drained while still very al dente and placed on a sheet of baking parchment or aluminum foil together with your chosen sauce, which should be rather liquid. The

sheet must then be closed carefully, with no gaps, creating the *cartoccio* (parcel), and placed on a sheet pan (baking tray) in the oven at 350°F (180°C/Gas Mark 4) for 15–20 minutes. This type of cooking is excellent for preserving the flavors of the ingredients, which blend perfectly with the pasta; the rich aromas then burst from the *cartoccio* when opened.

Another style of cooking that has been practiced with great energy recently is **pasta risottata**, the word risottata recalling the risotto cooking method that inspired it. Commonly used in restaurants, it is now also widespread in domestic kitchens and allows better fusion of the pasta with the sauce, increasing its creaminess. Heat a skillet (frying pan) and lightly toast the pasta before gradually adding the required amount of liquid, continuing to stir until all the liquid has been absorbed. The starch released from the pasta binds to the sauce, guaranteeing an excellent risotto-style dish.

The choice of shape and type of sauce are fundamental in risotto-style pasta. For thin pasta shapes, the hot cooking water is poured directly into the pan with the raw pasta. For thicker shapes, it is recommended you precook the pasta for about half of its cooking time before draining and proceeding as above, gradually adding the liquid, keeping the temperature constant, and stirring continuously, as you would for a regular risotto. Thanks to the starch released by the pasta, this technique helps to thicken and bind sauces that otherwise wouldn't amalgamate well. Spaghetti with clams is an excellent dish to make using this technique, as the starch facilitates the emulsion of the sauce.

Another method that has gained popularity over recent years is **passive cooking**, or cooking off the heat. This technique allows you to create excellent pasta dishes while saving energy and reducing the impact on the environment. Passive cooking begins after about 2 minutes of active cooking in boiling salted water, during which the pasta is stirred a few times. Once the heat has been turned off, the saucepan is covered with a lid until the cooking is complete, following roughly the time indicated in the packet instructions. The lid should not be removed as the temperature of the water must drop gradually and without any sudden change. A steel saucepan with a thick base is ideal, having good thermal inertia, and thus preventing the water from falling below 175°F/80°C. Passive cooking reduces carbon dioxide emissions by up to 80 per cent, and bearing in mind that all over the world around 400 million portions of pasta are served every day, if passive cooking were adopted by a majority of people, the impact on the planet would be considerable.

FUSILLONI SALAD WITH SALTED CODFISH, FAVA BEANS, AND OLIVES

The fava (broad) beans create a perfect union with the olives and salted codfish in a pasta salad that is simply sublime in the springtime, the season of this particular legume. Botticelli's *Primavera* in a bowl of pasta.

50 min   12 min

SERVES 4

11 oz/320 g bronze-drawn fusilloni or fusilli
⅓ cup plus 1 tablespoon (3½ fl oz/100 ml) extra virgin olive oil, plus extra for drizzling
1 bunch basil
1 clove garlic, chopped
8¾ oz/250 g salted codfish, soaked in water for 24 hours, and cut into pieces
vegetable broth (stock) (optional)
7 oz/200 g fresh (or frozen) fava (broad) beans, shelled
scant ⅓ cup (1¾ oz/50 g) pitted Taggiasca olives
6¼ oz/180 g vine tomatoes, peeled, deseeded, and diced (see page 26)
salt and freshly ground black pepper

Cook the pasta in plenty of salted, boiling water according to the packet instructions. When still very al dente, remove from the heat and chill it by passing it quickly under cold running water. Then drain, pour into a serving bowl and garnish with a drizzle of oil to stop it sticking.

Blend half of the oil with the basil, then strain the mixture through a fine-meshed sieve and put to one side.

Heat half of the remaining oil in a pan with the garlic clove for 1 minute. Add the codfish and salt and pepper to taste, and cook quickly to prevent the fish breaking up, 4–6 minutes. Moisten with a little vegetable broth (stock) if necessary.

Cook the fava (broad) beans in lightly salted, boiling water. Leave them to cool and remove their skins, then season with salt, pepper, and the remaining oil.

Add the fava beans, olives, tomatoes, and codfish to the pasta. Adjust salt and pepper to taste, and garnish with the basil oil.

Tip
You can substitute the codfish with the same quantity of monkfish for a more delicate dish.

MEZZI RIGATONI WITH SALTED CODFISH AND ZABAIONE

The marine flavor of the salted codfish is tempered by the water and the milk, but the salted zabaione of French origin is what gives it that touch of class. And both unite with the mezzi rigatoni, ready to be filled to the brim with a delicious creamy sauce.

1 hour   40 min

SERVES 4

11 oz/320 g bronze-drawn mezzi
    rigatoni or penne rigate
5 tablespoons extra virgin olive oil
2 cloves garlic, sliced
1 bunch parsley
⅔ cup (5 fl oz/150 ml) milk
3 tablespoons plus 1½ teaspoons
    double (heavy) cream
7 oz/200 g salted codfish, soaked
    in water for 24 hours, and cut
    into pieces
1 bay leaf (optional)
microgreens, to garnish (optional)
salt and freshly ground black
    pepper

FOR THE ZABAIONE
3 egg yolks
1¾ oz/50 g Parmigiano Reggiano,
    grated
freshly ground black pepper

Heat 3 tablespoons of oil in a pan with the garlic, some parsley sprigs, the milk, and cream for around 15 minutes on very low heat. Add salt and pepper to taste.

Cook the codfish and bay leaf, if using, in a pan of simmering water for around 30 minutes, then drain, retaining a little of the cooking water. In a blender, blend the fish gradually, adding the aromatic oil prepared above, along with a little of the codfish cooking liquid at the end, to lend the right texture; the codfish cream should not be too liquid.

Cook the pasta in plenty of salted, boiling water according to the packet instructions.

In the meantime, for the zabaione, beat the egg yolks, Parmigiano, and a little pepper over a bain marie, keeping the temperature below 150°F/65°C; if the mixture starts to lump too quickly, remove from the flame and continue beating. The zabaione is ready when it is foamy and smooth.

Drain the mezzi rigatoni when al dente, then garnish with the creamy codfish using a piping bag.

Spoon the pasta onto the plates and top with the zabaione. Garnish as you wish with microgreen sprouts and freshly ground black pepper.

Tip
The codfish cream used in this recipe is also perfect served with hot crostini.

SPAGHETTI QUADRATI WITH CLAMS, SALICORNIA, AND LIME

The salicornia (samphire) is in a play-off with the clams for the flavor of the sea, while the robust structure of the spaghetto quadrato lets them get on with it until finally making its presence known.

30 min   30 min

SERVES 4

14 oz/400 g bronze-drawn
    spaghetti quadrati or linguine
2 red bell peppers
6 tablespoons extra virgin olive oil
1 clove garlic
2½ lb/1.2kg clams, cleaned (see
    page 57)
2 tablespoons lemon juice
¾ oz/20 g salicornia (samphire),
    chopped
grated zest of 1 lime
salt and freshly ground black
    pepper

Preheat the oven to 400°F (200°C/Gas Mark 6).

Place the whole peppers in a baking dish and cook in the oven for 20 minutes. Once cooked, take the liquid released during cooking, transfer to a pan over high heat, and reduce it to around 4 tablespoons.

Heat 4 tablespoons of oil and the garlic in a pan over medium-high heat for a minute or so, then add the clams and cook for 3–4 minutes. Strain the cooking water, put to one side, then remove the clams from their shells and set aside.

Cook the pasta in plenty of salted, boiling water according to the packet instructions. Drain halfway through the cooking time indicated and transfer to a pan with the clam water, the pepper water reduction, and the lemon juice and cook for 5 minutes. Finally, blend to a cream with 2 tablespoons of oil.

Before serving, add the clams and some black pepper, and stir. Complete the plates with a little chopped salicornia (samphire) and the lime zest.

Tip
You can substitute the salicornia with the same quantity of chopped parsley. You can also use the roasted peppers as a starter, cut into pieces and garnished with oil, salt, vinegar, and parsley.

TORTIGLIONI WITH PARMIGIANO CREAM, TUNA, AND CAPERBERRIES

The ideal dish for a refined lunch, dedicated to gourmet friends who can appreciate the contrasting flavors.

40 min   15 min

SERVES 4

11 oz/320 g bronze-drawn tortiglioni or mezzi rigatoni

⅓ cup plus 1 tablespoon (3½ fl oz/100 ml) white wine

2 shallots, sliced

1¾ cups (14 fl oz/400 ml) heavy (double) cream

7 oz/200 g aged Parmigiano Reggiano, grated

3½ tablespoons (1¾ oz/50 g) butter

6⅓ pints/3 liters vegetable broth (stock)

1 teaspoon coffee powder

2¾ oz/80 g oil-packed tuna ventresca (belly)

oregano leaves, to garnish

caperberries, to garnish

For the cream, reduce the wine with the shallots for 5 minutes, then add the cream, Parmigiano, and the butter, and blend together.

Heat the vegetable broth (stock) in a pan to boiling, add the pasta, and cook until al dente. Drain, and mix into the Parmigiano cream.

Garnish with a light dusting of coffee, the tuna (broken up with your hands), a few fresh oregano leaves, and some caperberries, and serve

Tip

Is it possible to translate "umami" in a Mediterranean dish? This recipe, of a rather unusual union—at least for Italian cuisine—of cheese and fish, does just that: both elements reverberate with umami, which, when blended with the roasted notes of the coffee, becomes even stronger, while the caperberries lend a salty green nuance.

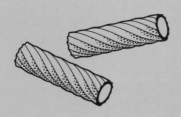

PARMIGIANO REGGIANO

Parmigiano Reggiano PDO (Protected Designation of Origin) is one of Italy's most renowned and ancient cheeses. It was around the year 1000 when the Benedictine monks started experimenting with the processing of cow's milk, a technique that was then consolidated over the centuries, and in 1955 it was given PDO recognition, underlining an unbreakable link with a well-defined area in the provinces of Parma, Reggio Emilia, Modena, and parts of Mantua and Bologna. Parmigiano Reggiano is produced with three essential ingredients: cow's milk, natural rennet, and rock salt, without additives or preservatives. It is aged for between twelve and thirty-six months, contributing to the formation of its grainy consistency and its rich and complex flavor. The result is a yellow cheese with a hard texture, a brown rind, and a slightly spicy flavor. The PDO label certifies its authenticity and compliance with these production specifications.

Parmigiano Reggiano owes its global success to its versatility: it can be used over pasta, in salads and soups, or consumed alone as an appetizer. Whatever its use, it remains a unique tasting experience and is one of the universal symbols of Italian gastronomic culture, loved and celebrated throughout the world. Even today the strictly artisanal production is handed down through the generations, and is very closely connected to the culinary history of Emilia-Romagna.

FUSILLI MARINATED IN GINGER AND DILL WITH SMOKED SALMON

1 h 20 min 10 min

SERVES 4

11 oz/320 g bronze-drawn fusilli or tortiglioni
¾ oz/20 g ginger, peeled and sliced
1¾ oz/50 g dill, plus extra to serve
1½ oz/40 g celery stalk, cut in diamonds
1 carrot, diced
1 red carrot, cut into rounds
3½ oz/100 g asparagus, thinly cut
2 small zucchini (courgettes), julienned
1¾ oz/50 g shelled peas
1¾ oz/50 g green beans
3½ oz/100 g smoked salmon, sliced
2 tablespoons extra virgin olive oil
salt and freshly ground black pepper

Put the ginger and dill in an extractor and put the liquid extracted to one side. Discard the solids.

Set aside the celery and carrot in iced water, so they stay crunchy.

Blanch all the other vegetables separately in a pan of salted, boiling water for 2 minutes, then drain and immerse in iced water. When cooled, drain and put into a large bowl.

Cook the pasta in plenty of salted, boiling water for 2 minutes less than the cooking time indicated on the packet. Drain, and cool quickly under cold running water.

Combine 4 tablespoons of the ginger and dill extract with 2 tablespoons of the oil. Put the pasta, salmon, and remaining ginger and dill extract in the bowl with the blanched vegetables. Adjust salt and pepper to taste and leave to marinate for around 1 hour.

Serve the dish with the carefully dried raw vegetables. Drizzle with the ginger and dill oil and scatter over a few dill leaves.

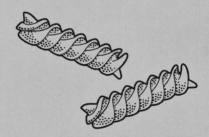

CONCHIGLIE RIGATE WITH LAMB AND SAFFRON RAGÙ

60 min   45 min

SERVES 4

11 oz/320 g bronze-drawn
   conchiglie rigate or mezzi
   rigatoni
4 tablespoons extra virgin olive oil
½ onion, diced
5 sage leaves, plus extra to
   garnish
12 oz/340 g ground (minced) lamb
1 cup (8 fl oz/250 ml) white wine
1 x 2 g sachet of saffron
1¾ oz/50 g Pecorino Romano,
   grated
salt and freshly ground black
   pepper

Heat the oil in a pan over medium heat and sauté the onion for 3–4 minutes until translucent.

Add the sage and the lamb and cook on high heat for 5 minutes until browned.

Add the white wine, and cook for 2–3 minutes until reduced and the alcohol has evaporated, then add 3 cups/750 ml of water, the saffron, and salt and pepper to taste. Reduce the heat to a simmer, and cook the ragù for around 30 minutes.

In the meantime, cook the pasta in plenty of salted, boiling water according to the packet instructions. Drain when al dente, retaining some of the cooking water, and mix the pasta into the pan with the lamb ragù once cooked, adding a little of the cooking water, if needed. Serve with a sprinkling of Pecorino and sage leaves.

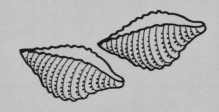

CONCHIGLIE RIGATE WITH FRIED EGGPLANT AND MEATBALLS

The fragrance of the fried eggplant (aubergine) and the warmth of the meatballs make this a recipe to enjoy for its immediacy and wholesomeness.

40 min   30 min

SERVES 4

311 oz/320 g bronze-drawn conchiglie or penne rigate

1 bread roll

3 tablespoons plus 1½ teaspoons milk

5¼ oz/150 g ground (minced) beef

2¾ oz/80 g Parmigiano Reggiano, grated

1 tablespoon finely chopped parsley

¼ cup (1 oz/30 g) all-purpose (plain) flour

6 tablespoons extra virgin olive oil, plus extra for drizzling

5¼ oz/150 g soffritto mix (finely diced celery stalk, carrot, and onion)

1 clove garlic, crushed

15¾ oz/450 g canned crushed tomatoes

5–6 basil leaves

10½ oz/300 g eggplant (aubergine), peeled and cut into ½-inch/1-cm cubes

vegetable oil, for frying

salt and freshly ground black pepper

Remove any crust from the bread roll and dunk the soft bread into the milk, squeeze out the liquid, chop the bread and put it in a bowl with the ground (minced) beef, one-third of the Parmigiano, the chopped parsley, and some salt and pepper. Knead the ingredients to combine, then form small meatballs with the mixture, dust with flour, and fry in a pan on medium heat with 4 tablespoons of oil until browned and cooked through, 5–6 minutes.

Heat the remaining oil in a pan over medium heat and fry the soffritto mix and garlic clove for 3–4 minutes until softened. Add the crushed tomatoes and salt and pepper to taste, increase the heat to high, and cook for around 10 minutes before adding the meatballs.

Heat some vegetable oil in a deep pan—enough to cover the eggplant (aubergine)—then fry the cubes of eggplant for 3–4 minutes, drain with a slotted spatula, and place on some paper towels.

Preheat the oven to 400°F (200°C/Gas Mark 6).

Cook the pasta in plenty of salted, boiling water according to the packet instructions. Drain when al dente and mix together with the sauce, the eggplant, and some ripped basil leaves. Pour into a baking dish, sprinkle with the remaining Parmigiano, drizzle with a little oil, and cook in the oven for 5–6 minutes.

Tip
For a lighter version of this recipe, cook the meatballs in the oven at 350°F (180°C/Gas Mark 4) for 10 minutes and sauté the eggplants rather than deep-frying them.

TORTIGLIONI WITH PANCETTA AND BLACK TRUFFLE

The unmistakable aroma of the truffle, the crunchy sweetness of the pancetta, the regality of the bronze-drawn tortiglione—intense fall (autumn) flavors to be shared.

15 min   10 min

SERVES 4

11 oz/320 g bronze-drawn
    tortiglioni or mezzi rigatoni
1 tablespoon extra virgin olive oil
8 oz/225 g pancetta, julienned
5 egg yolks
2½ oz/75 g Parmigiano Reggiano,
    grated
1 oz/30 g white truffle, cut into
    chips
salt and freshly ground black
    pepper

Cook the pasta in plenty of salted, boiling water according to the packet instructions.

In the meantime, heat the oil in a pan over medium heat and sauté the pancetta until crunchy.

In a separate bowl, mix the egg yolks, grated Parmigiano, and salt and black pepper to taste. Stir in 2–3 tablespoons of pasta cooking water to loosen the mixture.

Drain the pasta when al dente and sauté in the pan with the crunchy pancetta for 1 minute. Stir the egg yolk mixture into the pasta and stir well on low heat until the sauce starts to thicken; the egg must not be overcooked. Serve the tortiglioni garnished with the truffle chips.

Tip
For a more robust flavor, substitute the pancetta with the same amount of guanciale (cheek lard), following the recipe above.

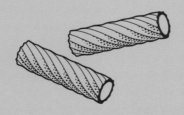

EMBRACING CREATIVITY

ANCIENT AND MODERN DESIGNS OF TASTE

What if it wasn't just a question of creativity but of widespread genius? Dario Fo, playwright and Nobel Prize winner for Literature, used to call young students on stage to improvise. As they took to the stage, they would think of something sensible to recite, but often they would merely utter empty or uninspiring sentences. "Use your dialect," Fo would urge. "But what if they don't understand?" the students objected. "They will understand the rhythm of emotions," Fo replied.

Dialect is not just a variant of language, it is the very essence of a people or territory; it is the most ancestral and intimate connection. For this reason, many pasta shapes have been given names from different dialects, as if to validate the profound link between identity and everyday food. One example is cavatelli—*cavatielle* in the Molise dialect—small durum wheat semolina dumplings, whose name derives from their typical hollowed shape, which is ideal for collecting the sauce; it is a handmade pasta of ancient origins, which has spread throughout Southern Italy since the times of Frederick II of Swabia. And then there's ziti, which in Southern dialects is a term used to indicate engaged couples: similar to bucatini, but larger in diameter, it was served in the past during engagement parties. Imagine the scene: a boy and a girl, shy and excited, surrounded by the noise of their celebrating family members, while overflowing plates of ziti are passed from hand to hand.

The best-known pasta shapes are naturally the most widespread, yet there is a goldmine of complexity and richness made up of over three hundred shapes—all made in Italy—creating a truly unique mosaic of varieties throughout the world. They are ancient examples of design, which, over the centuries, have become emblematic of the multifaceted ingenuity of pasta. Among them are corzetti, a type of Ligurian pasta from the fourteenth century shaped like a large coin, which at the time featured the coat of arms of the family or noble house where they were made imprinted on the surface by a special wooden mold. And bigoli, large rustic spaghetti with a rough surface, named after the "bigolaro," a cylindrical press found in almost all houses in the Veneto.

Catalogued by size or dominant characteristic, pasta shapes are divided into full and hollow, short and long, smooth and ridged, regular and irregular—alongside many others. From the very beginning, master pasta makers wanted to create pasta in refined, delicious, and spectacular shapes. Perhaps they were driven by romantic motives, or perhaps by pure narcissism or artistic egocentrism—yet not infrequently, those formats that enhance the *genius loci*, those which today we would define as regional specialities, were not only created by the pursuit of something new or a need to amaze. The geometry of taste has ancient and rather rigorous rules: it requires that each pasta shape has an elective affinity with a specific sauce, able to fully bring out its best properties. Could we really imagine trofie without Genoese pesto, or orecchiette without cime di rapa (broccoli rabe)? The final impression depends on the successful interaction between shape and sauce. The right sauce used to garnish the wrong shape would not make for a satisfying taste experience.

The pasta shapes that have passed into tradition are those that have proved successful, often due to the ingenious brilliance of their shape. The forerunners of today's copywriters indulged themselves by observing nature in their poetic naming of shapes, hence we have farfalle, lumachine, conchigliette, or even midolline (from melon seeds), and risoni (grains of rice with an elongated shape). And in more recent times, acclaimed international designers have turned their hand to it, combining their undeniable visionary talent with the functionality necessary for a product, such as pasta, which must satisfy all the senses. The trefoil section of the trigatelli and their strategically lined surface, as well as the enveloping scrolls of papiri belong to this strand of design. It's true you should be thinking of your palate, but the other senses also need to be satisfied.

In the film *When Harry Met Sally,* brilliant screenwriter Nora Ephron has Harry order "number 3" from the menu, while Sally drives the waiter crazy with a long list of variations. And similarly, the Italians, over the centuries, have shaped their own fantasies, because tradition is fine, but change is irresistible and necessary. Over 150 years of corporate history, Barilla has been able to gather and pay homage to many regional pasta shapes. It's a repertoire that is enriched every year with new styles, and limited or special editions, using the contributions of designers and artists. Or by taking up those regional formats, forgotten over time, and giving them new life. Regional recipes are the profound spirit of a territory; they are all those differences that make Italy a country worth discovering.

The rediscovery of traditions is not just about nostalgia for the past—quite the contrary, it is the prerequisite for innovation. The journey of pasta must continue thanks to new codes of creativity. Think of Giambattista Bodoni, an entire life spent as a royal typographer in eighteenth-century Parma, who went down in history for inventing a graphic character that is unique in its elegance, sharpness, and absolute modernity. The same is true of pasta: the hundreds of shapes that we have at our fingertips today are an important legacy, one that deserves to be rediscovered and appreciated in the name of taste—including a taste for beauty and gastronomic passion. The different shapes featured in these recipes will help you to create some truly special moments.

FUSILLI BUCATI CORTI WITH PEAR, GORGONZOLA, AND WALNUTS

15 min   20 min

SERVES 4

11 oz/320 g fusilli bucati corti
   or casarecce
2 pears, peeled, cored, and diced,
   plus a few thin slices to garnish
juice of 1 lemon
4¼ oz/120 g Gorgonzola,
   cut into pieces
8 shelled walnuts, coarsely
   chopped
2 sprigs fresh thyme, leaves picked
salt

Baste the diced pears with the lemon juice to stop them from becoming discolored.

Cook the pasta in plenty of salted, boiling water according to the packet instructions. Drain when al dente, then transfer to a pan with the Gorgonzola, pears, walnuts, and thyme leaves and sauté for a few minutes until warmed through. Garnish each plate with a few thin slices of pear, and serve.

Tip
Choose a cooking pear for this recipe, such as Decana, Kaiser, Bosc, or D'Anjou, as they remain solid.

FUSILLI BUCATI CORTI WITH VEGETABLES AND CACIOCAVALLO

50 min   35 min

SERVES 4

11 oz/320 g fusilli bucati corti
   or orecchiette
2 eggplants (aubergines): 1 thinly
   sliced, 1 diced
vegetable oil, for frying
2 tablespoons extra virgin olive oil
1¼ oz/50 g carrots, diced
1¼ oz/50 g mix of yellow and red
   bell peppers, diced
3½ oz/100 g tomato, diced
3½ oz/100 g zucchini (courgettes),
   diced
1 teaspoon chopped parsley
5¼ oz/150 g caciocavallo, diced
1¼ oz/50 g Parmigiano Reggiano,
   grated
salt and freshly ground black
   pepper

FOR THE BÉCHAMEL
2¾ tablespoons (1½ oz/40 g)
   butter
⅓ cup (1½ oz/40 g) all-purpose
   (plain) flour
2 cups (17 fl oz/500 ml) milk,
   boiling
whole nutmeg, for grating
salt

Place the eggplant (aubergine) slices in a colander, sprinkle with salt, and leave for around 30 minutes until they discard all their liquids.

Heat plenty of vegetable oil in a pan and fry the eggplant slices.

Heat the extra virgin olive oil in a separate pan and sauté all the diced vegetables with the parsley and salt and pepper to taste for 10 minutes.

In the meantime, prepare the béchamel: melt the butter in a pan over low heat, add the flour, and leave to cook for 3–4 minutes, stirring constantly with a whisk. Gradually add the boiling milk, salt, and a grating of nutmeg and continue cooking, stirring constantly to avoid clumps, until you get a thick, creamy sauce.

Cook the pasta in plenty of salted, boiling water, and drain 1–2 minutes before the end of the cooking time indicated on the packet. Stir through the vegetables, the béchamel, and the caciocavallo.

Preheat the oven to 365°F (185°C/Gas Mark 5).

Divide the fried eggplant slices among 4 round ovenproof dishes, overlapping them slightly and allowing them to drape over the edge, and fill with the pasta mixture. Sprinkle with the grated Parmigiano, cover with the eggplant slices, and cook in the oven for 15–20 minutes until the surface is nicely gratinéed.

CASARECCE AU GRATIN WITH RADICCHIO AND MASCARPONE

 30 min   35 min

SERVES 4

11 oz/320 g casarecce or fusilli
2 tablespoons extra virgin olive oil
17⅔ oz/500 g red radicchio, cut
　into strips
3½ oz/100 g leeks, sliced
⅓ cup plus 1 tablespoon
　(3½ fl oz/100 ml) red wine
1 sprig thyme
1 oz/30 g Parmigiano Reggiano,
　grated
salt

FOR THE SAUCE
1 tablespoon (½ oz/15 g) butter
⅛ cup (½ oz/15 g) all-purpose
　(plain) flour
1¼ cups (10½ fl oz/300 ml) milk,
　boiling
whole nutmeg, for grating
7 oz/200 g mascarpone
salt

Heat the oil in a pan over medium heat. Add the radicchio and leeks and cook for 5 minutes. Add the red wine and leave to evaporate for 3–4 minutes. Add the thyme and leave to cook for 15 minutes.

For the sauce, melt the butter in a pan, then add the flour, stir well, and pour in the boiling milk with a pinch of salt and a grating of nutmeg. Bring to the boil, stirring constantly, add the mascarpone, and put to one side.

Cook the pasta in plenty of salted, boiling water according to the packet instructions. Drain when al dente, and garnish with the radicchio and sauce.

Preheat the oven to 350°F (180°C/Gas Mark 4).

Put everything into an oven dish, sprinkle with the Parmigiano, and cook for 10 minutes, or until golden on top.

Tip
You can swap the radicchio for spinach or zucchini (courgettes) cut into rounds, and follow the recipe above.

FARFALLE WITH TREVISANO RADICCHIO AND HAZELNUTS

30 min   12 min

SERVES 4

11 oz/320 g farfalle or casarecce

2 teaspoons extra virgin olive oil

¾ oz/20 g white onion, thinly
   sliced

3½ oz/100 g Trevisano radicchio,
   finely chopped

¾ oz/20 g basil leaves

⅛ cup (¾ oz/20 g) hazelnuts,
   chopped

salt and freshly ground
   black pepper

Heat the extra virgin olive oil in a pan and cook the onion for 2–3 minutes. Add the Trevisano radicchio and cook for a further 2–3 minutes, adding salt and pepper to taste.

Cook the pasta in plenty of salted, boiling water according to the packet instructions. Drain when al dente and transfer to the pan with the sautéed radicchio, adding most of the basil.

Serve the pasta garnished with a few ripped basil leaves and the chopped hazelnuts.

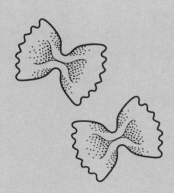

TAGLIOLINI WITH TRUFFLE

10 min 10 min

SERVES 4

8¾ oz/250 g tagliolini paglia
  e fieno or egg tagliatelle
3½ tablespoons (1¾ oz/50 g)
  butter
1½ oz/40 g truffle, thinly sliced
salt

Cook the pasta in plenty of salted, boiling water according to the packet instructions.

In the meantime, melt the butter in a pan and add 1 ladleful of the pasta cooking water.

Drain the tagliolini when al dente, then sauté in the butter for 2 minutes. Sprinkle the truffle slices directly over the pasta while serving.

EGG PAPPARDELLE WITH PORCINI MUSHROOMS

20 min   10 min

SERVES 4

8¾ oz/250 g egg pappardelle or
  egg tagliatelle
2 tablespoons extra virgin olive oil
1 clove garlic, chopped
2 tablespoons chopped parsley
14 oz/400 g porcini mushrooms,
  cleaned and sliced (see Tip)
1 tablespoon plus 1 teaspoon white
  wine
salt and freshly ground black
  pepper

Heat the oil in a pan and fry the garlic and parsley for
1–2 minutes. Add the mushrooms and cook for around
5 minutes, so they remain intact. Pour in the white wine
and add salt and pepper to taste.

Cook the pasta in plenty of salted, boiling water according
to the packet instructions. Drain when al dente, and pour
into the pan with the mushrooms. Stir well and cook for
another 2 minutes.

Tip
For the perfect porcini sauce, the secret is in the cleaning
and cooking. Never wash the mushrooms under running
water; in order to remove all impurities and dirt, just brush
them very gently with some damp paper towels. Cook them
in a very hot nonstick pan with a drizzle of oil. During the
cooking, only turn the porcini over when they have formed
a light crust where in contact with the pan.

EGG LASAGNE ALLA GENOVESE

35 min   35 min

SERVES 4

8 sheets egg lasagne
3½ oz/100 g potatoes, thinly sliced
1¾ oz/50 g green beans, cut
   into rounds

FOR THE PESTO
scant ¼ cup (1 oz/25 g) pine nuts
1 clove garlic
2⅔ oz/75 g basil leaves
2¾ tablespoons extra virgin olive
   oil, plus extra if needed
1 oz/25 g Pecorino Romano,
   grated
2½ oz/70 g Parmigiano Reggiano,
   grated

FOR THE BÉCHAMEL
2 tablespoons (1 oz/30 g) butter
⅓ cup (¾ oz/25 g) all-purpose
   (plain) flour
2 cups (17 fl oz/500 ml) milk,
   boiling
salt

For the pesto, put the pine nuts and garlic into a blender and blend. Add the basil and oil with the blender still on. Then add the Pecorino and 1¾ oz/50 g of the Parmigiano and adjust the thickness by adding more oil if necessary.

Cook the potatoes and beans in a pan of boiling water until al dente, and drain.

For the béchamel, melt the butter in a pan over low heat, add the flour, and leave to cook for 3–4 minutes, stirring constantly with a whisk. Gradually add the boiling milk and salt to taste, and continue cooking, stirring constantly to avoid clumps, until you get a thick, creamy sauce.

Preheat the oven to 340°F (170°C/Gas Mark 3).

For the lasagne, spread a little béchamel, pesto, green beans, and potatoes on the bottom of a baking dish and cover with 2 sheets of pasta side by side. Repeat the procedure a further 3 times until you have 4 layers. Cover the final layer with the béchamel and complete with the remaining grated Parmigiano.

Put in the oven for 20–25 minutes until golden and bubbling. Leave to rest for 5 minutes before serving.

Tip
For a dish that is chromatically richer in vegetable harmony, use green egg lasagne.

PECORINO ROMANO

Pecorino Romano PDO (Protected Designation of Origin) is an Italian cheese of centuries-old tradition, produced in the Grosseto area, in Lazio, and in Sardinia. The PDO attests to the traditional production methods and geographical origin of the cheese, preserving its authenticity and excellence. Its origins date back to Ancient Rome, when it was an integral part of the daily diet of legionaries due to it being easily preserved and rich in protein.

Pecorino Romano is obtained exclusively from sheep's milk from designated areas. The curd mass—created after the addition of the rennet to milk—is cut and pressed before being placed into molds. It is then left to age, from five months to over a year.

The cheese is hard and has a white-ivory appearance with a dry and grainy structure, while the external surface is covered with a brown-black wax. The flavor varies in intensity, from sweet and delicate, to aromatic and spicy. Tradition dictates that this cheese is grated or broken into flakes and used to garnish dishes such as Cacio e Pepe or the famous pasta all'Amatriciana. With its strong taste and unique texture, Pecorino Romano has become an icon of Italian cuisine.

SPAGHETTI FRITTATA WITH ZUCCHINI AND PARMIGIANO

30 min   35 min

SERVES 4

7 oz/200 g Spaghetti n. 5
   or bucatini
4 eggs
¾ oz/20 g Parmigiano Reggiano,
   grated
1 tablespoon extra virgin olive oil
7 oz/200 g zucchini (courgettes),
   cut into rounds
1 shallot, chopped
salt and freshly ground
   black pepper

In a mixing bowl, beat the eggs with a pinch of salt, the Parmigiano, and a grinding of black pepper.

Heat the oil in a pan over medium heat and sauté the zucchini (courgettes) with the shallot for 3–4 minutes.

In the meantime, cook the pasta in plenty of salted, boiling water according to the packet instructions. Drain when al dente, and pour into a bowl, stirring in the beaten eggs and zucchini. Add salt and pepper to taste.

Preheat the oven to 300°F (150°C/Gas Mark 2).

Pour the mixture into an ovenproof pan or baking dish and cook for 20 minutes, or until the frittata is set.

Remove from the oven and cut the frittata into slices or small cubes and serve.

PAPIRI WITH CREAM OF BROCCOLI AND AROMATIC BREAD CRUMBS

30 min   20 min

SERVES 4

11 oz/320 g papiri or fusilli bucati corti
2 tablespoons extra virgin olive oil
1 clove garlic, peeled and whole
3 slices fresh bread (without the crust), crumbled
7 oz/200 g broccoli
1 chili pepper, sliced, plus extra to serve
5 anchovy fillets in oil
salt

Heat 1 tablespoon of oil in a pan with the garlic clove for 1–2 minutes, to flavor the oil.

Add the bread and toast until golden and crunchy, then put to one side.

Separate the broccoli florets from the stalks and cut the stalks into rounds about the same size as the florets so they can be cooked together.

Heat the remaining oil in the same pan you used for the bread and add the same garlic clove and the sliced chili pepper. Leave to flavor for 2 minutes, then add all the broccoli and 1 ladleful of boiling water and cook until tender, about 10 minutes. Finally, add the anchovy fillets and cook for 5 minutes until they have broken up. Leave to cool slightly, then blend everything in a small blender, adding salt to taste if necessary.

In the meantime, cook the pasta in plenty of salted, boiling water according to the packet instructions. Drain when al dente and pour into the pan with the broccoli cream. Serve with a sprinkling of crunchy bread and sliced chili pepper, to taste.

Tip
In summer, you can use frozen broccoli, or substitute with seasonal vegetables such as zucchini (courgettes), following the recipe above.

PAPIRI WITH VERMOUTH, APRICOTS, AND CREAM OF PARMIGIANO

30 min   15 min

SERVES 4

11 oz/320 g papiri or
    mezzi rigatoni
⅓ cup plus 1 tablespoon
    (3½ fl oz/100 ml)
    Vermouth
1 tablespoon soy sauce
1¼ cups (10 fl oz/300 ml) heavy
    (double) cream
5¼ oz/150 g Parmigiano Reggiano,
    grated
extra virgin olive oil, for
    drizzling
5 dried apricots, sliced
pink peppercorns, to
    garnish
salt

Heat the Vermouth in a pan over low heat and leave to reduce until almost a syrup. Add the soy sauce for more intensity.

Put the cream in a small saucepan over low heat. Add the Parmigiano and heat until the cheese melts. Pass the mix through a sieve to get a smooth sauce.

Cook the pasta in plenty of salted, boiling water according to the packet instructions. Drain when al dente, reserving some of the cooking water, transfer to a clean pan, and stir for 10 seconds with a drizzle of oil and a little of the cooking water.

Spoon the papiri into pasta bowls and garnish with the Parmigiano cream, a few drops of Vermouth and soy sauce mixture, the apricots, and the pink peppercorns crumbled with your fingers.

FOUR-CHEESE PAPIRI

20 min   10 min

SERVES 4

11 oz/320 g papiri or orecchiette
3½ oz/100 g butter
2¾ oz/80 g Gorgonzola, cut into
    pieces
2¾ oz/80 g Edam, cut into pieces
2¾ oz/80 g Gruyère, cut into
    pieces
3½ oz/100 g Parmigiano Reggiano:
    half cut into pieces, half grated
salt and freshly ground black
    pepper

Melt the butter in a small saucepan over low heat and keep warm.

In the meantime, cook the pasta in plenty of salted, boiling water according to the packet instructions. Drain when al dente, and garnish with the cut cheeses, half the melted butter, and half the grated Parmigiano.

Divide the pasta between 4 plates and add the remaining grated Parmigiano and butter.

Serve immediately, with a grinding of pepper, before the four cheeses blend together completely.

TRIGATELLI WITH CARAMELIZED CHERRY TOMATOES, GOAT'S CHEESE, AND PINE NUTS

20 min   1 hour

SERVES 4

11 oz/320 g trigatelli or rigatoni
7 oz/200 g Pachino tomatoes
1 tablespoon brown sugar
1 sprig thyme
1 tablespoon plus 1½ teaspoons
   grated citrus zest (orange and
   lemon), plus extra to serve
1 tablespoon plus 1 teaspoon extra
   virgin olive oil, plus extra for
   drizzling
1 oz/30 g scallions (spring onions),
   sliced
1½ oz/40 g fresh goat's cheese,
   plus extra to serve
generous ⅛ cup (¾ oz/20 g)
   pine nuts, toasted
salt

Preheat the oven to 250°F (120°C/Gas Mark ½).

Place the tomatoes on a sheet pan (baking tray), with the sugar, thyme, citrus zest, a drizzle of oil, and some salt, and cook for 1 hour.

Heat the oil in a pan over low heat and brown the scallions (spring onions) for around 5 minutes. Add the confit tomatoes and salt to taste.

Cook the pasta in plenty of salted, boiling water according to the packet instructions. Drain when al dente, and add to the pan of tomatoes together with the goat's cheese and pine nuts.

Serve the pasta with more citrus zest and goat's cheese to taste.

TRIGATELLI WITH CHAMPIGNON MUSHROOMS AND THYME ON A GORGONZOLA FONDUE

30 min   15 min

SERVES 4

11 oz/320 g trigatelli or cellentani
3 tablespoons extra virgin olive oil
chopped parsley, leaves and
    stalks divided
1 clove garlic, peeled and whole
14 oz/400 g champignon
    mushrooms, diced
1 sprig thyme, leaves picked
5¼ oz/150 g Gorgonzola
2 tablespoons heavy (double)
    cream
1¾ oz/50 g Parmigiano Reggiano,
    grated
1 oz/30 g mixed nuts, coarsely
    chopped (pistachios, hazelnuts,
    pine nuts)
salt and white pepper

Heat the oil with the parsley stalks and garlic clove in a pan over medium heat for 1–2 minutes, then add the mushrooms, increase the heat to high, and sauté for 3–4 minutes. When the mushrooms are nicely browned, discard the parsley stalks and garlic clove. Add salt and pepper to taste, along with most of the thyme leaves and the chopped parsley leaves.

Heat the Gorgonzola and cream in a saucepan over low heat; when the cheese has melted, add the Parmigiano and salt to taste. At this point, blend everything using an immersion blender and keep warm.

Cook the pasta in plenty of salted, boiling water according to the packet instructions. Drain when al dente, and sauté for a few seconds in the pan with the mushrooms.

While the pasta is cooking, toast the chopped nuts in a dry skillet (frying pan) for 2–3 minutes.

Spread a layer of Gorgonzola fondue in each pasta bowl and lay the pasta in the center. Before serving, garnish with the toasted nuts and remaining thyme leaves.

TROFIE WITH PESTO ALLA GENOVESE

20 min   10 min

SERVES 4

11 oz/320 g trofie or linguine
1 oz/30 g basil leaves
generous ¾ cup (7 fl oz/200 ml)
    extra virgin olive oil (from
    Liguria, if possible), plus extra
    to drizzle
1 clove garlic, peeled and whole
1 tablespoon pine nuts
2 oz/60 g Parmigiano Reggiano,
    grated
1½ oz/40 g Pecorino Romano,
    grated
3½ oz/100 g green beans, cut into
    pieces
7 oz/200 g potatoes, peeled and
    cut into ½-inch/1-cm cubes
salt

In a blender or mini food processor, blend the basil with ⅔ cup (5 fl oz/150 ml) oil, a pinch of salt, the garlic, and pine nuts. Then add the Parmigiano and Pecorino and blend again until you have a pesto consistency. Set to one side.

Cook the green beans, potatoes, and pasta in plenty of salted, boiling water. Drain when the pasta is al dente, reserving a little of the pasta cooking water, and transfer to a serving bowl. Garnish with the pesto, loosening it with some of the cooking water if needed, and a drizzle of oil.

TROFIE, AND THE STORY OF LIGURIA

Sori, Avegno, Recco, and Camogli: four villages overlooking the Ligurian sea, in the north-west of Italy, not far from Genoa, and the birthplace of trofie—a pasta small in size, with an elongated, intertwined, and thin shape with two tapered ends. Trofie with Genoese pesto is a dish everyone must try at least once in their lifetime—an excellence of Italian cuisine and the most universally known and appreciated Ligurian dish.

THE UNCERTAIN ORIGINS OF THE NAME

According to one scholarly interpretation, the name "trofia" may derive from the Greek trophe, which means nourishment. Another theory links the name to the Genoese *strufuggià* (to rub), which is the movement made with the hand in order to curl the dough on the cutting board. *The Italian Etymological Dictionary* of Carlo Battisti and Giovanni Alessio (1957) traces the name back to the words *tronfio* (pompous) or *gonfio* (swollen), while others still refer to the Latin *torquere* (to twist). Ultimately, there are no certainties about the origin of the name of this pasta with its small size and twisted shape.

A RECENT SUCCESS

Trofie began as a homemade product, prepared with durum wheat semolina and water and eaten at home or, at most, served in the trattorias of Sori, Avegno, Recco and Camogli. The unique aspect of this story is that, until the 1950s, trofie remained limited to these four villages and was practically unknown elsewhere. It was all under the control of local flour producers, talented housewives, and small shopkeepers who would sell it in shops or supply small restaurants throughout the area. In the 1970s, trade was extended to nearby Genoa, where the term "trofie" had always indicated gnocchi.

The success of trofie—as great as it was unexpected—risked creating havoc in the old domestic production system, and it was then that Bacci Cavassa, whose family ran a pasta factory in Sori, had the idea of creating a machine to mechanize the production process. Aided by some local artisans, Cavassa conceived and created a prototype, which he then refined over months until it produced trofie very similar to those made by the expert hands of the village housewives who used wooden knitting needles. The machine came into operation in 1977 at the Pastificio Novella company in Sori.

Dry production—allowing for ease of transport and preservation—has aided the export of trofie throughout the world. It is a success that has gone hand in hand with the rise in popularity of Genoese pesto in recent decades.

MAFALDINE WITH ESCAROLE AND OLIVES

20 min   10 min

SERVES 4

11 oz/320 g mafaldine or
   orecchiette
2 tablespoons extra virgin olive oil
3½ oz/100 g red onion,
   finely chopped
14 oz/400 g escarole,
   ripped into pieces
1 teaspoon dried oregano
25 pitted black olives,
   cut into pieces
3 tablespoons grated Pecorino
   Romano
salt and white pepper

In a nonstick skillet (frying pan), heat the oil and cook the onion for 3–4 minutes until softened. Add the escarole leaves and cook for a few minutes to soften, then add the oregano and black olives, and adjust salt and pepper to taste.

In the meantime, cook the pasta in plenty of salted, boiling water according to the packet instructions. Drain when al dente, and transfer to the skillet to sauté for a couple of minutes with the vegetables. Serve with a dusting of grated Pecorino.

ORECCHIETTE PUGLIESI WITH CIME DI RAPA

15 min   12 min

SERVES 4

11 oz/320 g orecchiette or
    casarecce
4 tablespoons extra virgin olive oil
1 clove garlic, thinly sliced
1 fresh red chili pepper, chopped
2 oil-packed anchovy fillets
10½ oz/300 g cime di rapa
    (broccoli rabe)
salt and freshly ground black
    pepper

Heat 3 tablespoons of oil in a wide, shallow pan and fry the garlic, chilli pepper, and anchovy fillets for 2–3 minutes, then add a few tablespoons of water and remove the pan from the heat.

In the meantime, cook the pasta together with the cime di rapa in plenty of salted, boiling water according to the packet instructions.

Drain the orecchiette when al dente, using a fine-meshed sieve to retain all the cime di rapa as well as the pasta. Pour everything into the pan with the anchovy sauce and stir. Add the remaining oil and a grinding of fresh pepper and serve.

CIME DI RAPA

Cime di rapa—also known as broccoli rabe—is a green, leafy cruciferous vegetable belonging to the Brassicaceae family. It has spiky, crunchy leaves, similar to those of cabbage, and a thin, fleshy central stem. The plant also produces small, edible yellow flower buds, which add a decorative and tasty touch to dishes. Of Mediterranean origin, and particularly widespread in the traditional cuisine of southern Italy, it is harvested before it has completely bloomed, while the leaves are young and tender.

Cime di rapa is a rich source of vitamins, especially A, C, and K, and also contains fiber and essential minerals such as calcium and iron. Very versatile in the kitchen, it can be found in numerous side dishes, soups, and stews—the flavor is slightly bitter, lending itself to a myriad of preparations, and making it a perfect accompaniment to spicy chili pepper. It found fame thanks to the Puglian specialty in which the leaves and buds of cime di rapa, together with garlic and chili pepper, are paired with orecchiette.

RISOTTO-STYLE LINGUINE WITH DANDELION, LANGOUSTINES, AND LEMON

80 min   30 min

SERVES 4

11 oz/320 g linguine or tagliolini
    paglia e fieno
1 oz/25 g dandelion leaves
7 oz/200 g langoustine tails
2 tablespoons (1 oz/30 g) butter
grated of zest of 1 Sorrento
    or unwaxed lemon
edible flowers and leaves of your
    choice, to garnish
salt and freshly ground
    black pepper

FOR THE AROMATIC OIL
3 tablespoons plus 1½
    teaspoons extra virgin
    olive oil
½ oz/15 g red garlic
⅙ oz/5 g fresh red chili pepper

FOR THE LANGOUSTINE WATER
7 langoustine shells
1¾ tablespoons extra virgin
    olive oil
3½ oz/100 g cherry tomatoes
3½ oz/100 g ice
⅛ oz/3 g basil leaves

For the aromatic oil, heat the oil in a pan to 140°F/60°C, then add the garlic and chili pepper and continue to cook at this temperature for 5 minutes. Strain, discarding the solids, and set to one side.

For the langoustine water, break the langoustine shells and toast them in a pan with the oil and cherry tomatoes for 2–3 minutes. When browned, add the ice for a thermal shock, then add 1¾ cups (14 fl oz/400 ml) water and cook on medium heat until boiling, every so often removing the foam that forms. Once boiling, remove from the heat, add the basil leaves, ripping them with your fingers, and quickly strain the liquid, being careful not to let the basil leaves blacken. Set to one side.

Quickly blanch the dandelion leaves in salted, boiling water for 20 seconds, then drain and plunge into iced water.

Pour the langoustine water into a wide pan and add the linguine, fanned out. Cook over low heat, gradually adding a little boiling water at a time until al dente.

Remove the pasta from the heat and add the blanched dandelion leaves and raw langoustine tails. Finally, add the aromatic oil and the butter, mixing well. Adjust salt and pepper to taste and add the lemon zest. Serve, garnished with edible flowers and leaves.

Tip
You can substitute the dandelion with the same quantities of finely chopped chives or some wild fennel.

LINGUINE WITH CUTTLEFISH INK, SHRIMP, AND 'NDUJA

30 min 15 min

SERVES 4

11 oz/320 g linguine or orecchiette
5 tablespoons extra virgin olive oil
2 cloves garlic
1 tablespoon chopped parsley
4 tablespoons 'nduja
15¾ oz/450 g medium shrimp
  (prawn) tails
½ cup (4 fl oz/120 ml) white wine
8¾ oz/250 g cherry tomatoes,
  halved
2 tablespoons cuttlefish ink
salt

Heat 2 tablespoons of oil in a pan and sauté the garlic for 1 minute. Add half the parsley, 2 tablespoons of 'nduja, and the shrimp (prawn) tails and sauté for 2 minutes.

Pour in the white wine and leave for 2 minutes until reduced by half. Add the cherry tomatoes, sauté for a few seconds, then add the cuttlefish ink and leave to reduce, about 2 minutes.

Cook the pasta in plenty of salted, boiling water according to the packet instructions.

In the meantime, in a separate pan, sauté the remaining 'nduja for 2 minutes in the remaining oil.

Drain the pasta when al dente, then stir into the shrimp sauce. Top with the sautéed 'nduja, and garnish with the remaining chopped parsley before serving.

Tip
Substitute the 'nduja, a very spicy Calabrian spreadable sausage, with 1 tablespoon of chopped dried chili peppers for a more delicate flavor.

LINGUINE WITH WHITE CLAM SAUCE

20 min   12 min

SERVES 4

11 oz/320 g linguine or orecchiette
2 lb 3 oz/1 kg clams (or wedge
    clams), cleaned (see page 57)
⅓ cup plus 1 tablespoon (3½ fl
    oz/100 ml) extra virgin olive oil
1 clove garlic, chopped
1 tablespoon chopped parsley
salt and freshly ground black
    pepper

Carefully wash the clams and put them in a large pan with
1 tablespoon of oil. Cover with a lid and put over medium
heat. Leave to sauté for 2–3 minutes and, once open, remove
from the heat and discard some of the shells. Strain the
cooking liquid, then pour back into the pan with the clams
and put everything to one side.

Heat the remaining oil in another pan and add the garlic.
Cook for 1–2 minutes, and when browned add the clams
with their liquid and simmer for 4–5 minutes. Adjust salt
and pepper to taste.

In the meantime, cook the pasta in plenty of salted, boiling
water according to the packet instructions. Drain when al
dente, reserving some of the cooking water, then cook for
a couple of minutes in the clam sauce, adding as much of
the cooking water as needed to loosen the sauce. Garnish
with the parsley.

PAPIRI WITH PROSECCO AND OYSTERS

25 min   12 min

SERVES 4

11 oz/320 g papiri or linguine
12 oysters
⅓ cup (3 fl oz/80 ml) extra virgin
   olive oil
2 small shallots, chopped
1 cup (8½ fl oz/250 ml) Prosecco
½ cup (4 ¼ fl oz/125 ml) fish broth
   (stock)
1½ cups/370 ml cooking (single)
   cream
3½ oz/100 g black caviar
12 sprigs chives
salt and white pepper

Open the oysters, separate the liquid, and put to one side.

Cook the pasta in plenty of salted, boiling water according to the packet instructions.

In the meantime, heat 3 tablespoons of oil in a pan over medium heat and soften the chopped shallots for 2–3 minutes. Add the Prosecco and leave to reduce by half. Add the oyster liquid and fish broth (stock), bring to the boil, and leave to reduce by half again. Add the cream, season with salt and white pepper, and leave to simmer.

Drain the pasta 2 minutes before the cooking time indicated—reserving 1 cup (8½ fl oz/250 ml) of the cooking water—and mix the pasta into the sauce, adding a little of the cooking water, if needed.

Stir in the oysters and cook for 2 minutes on medium heat to reduce the sauce and cook the oysters.

Serve the papiri garnished with the caviar, a drizzle of oil, and sprinkled with the chives.

FARFALLE WITH SALMON AND FENNEL

20 min   10 min

SERVES 4

11 oz/320 g farfalle or orecchiette
3 tablespoons extra virgin olive oil
3½ oz/100 g onion, finely chopped
1 fennel bulb, cut into ½-inch/1 cm
   cubes
1 lb/450 g salmon fillet, diced
salt and freshly ground black
   pepper

Heat the oil in a pan on low heat, add the onion and cook for 2 minutes. Add the fennel and leave to brown for 5 minutes. Increase the heat to high, add the diced salmon, then cook for 2 minutes, adding salt and pepper to taste.

In the meantime, cook the pasta in plenty of salted, boiling water according to the packet instructions. Drain when al dente, then transfer to the pan of sauce and cook for 1 minute to incorporate the sauce.

Tip
You can substitute the fresh salmon with 8¾–10 oz/250–300 g smoked salmon. In this case, simmer the salmon with ⅓ cup (3 fl oz/80 ml) white wine until reduced.

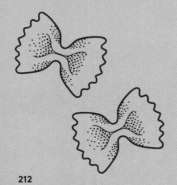

ORECCHIETTE WITH SEAFOOD SAUCE

45 min   30 min

SERVES 4

11 oz/320 g orecchiette or linguine
⅓ cup plus 1 tablespoon (3½ fl
   oz/100 ml) extra virgin olive oil
1 clove garlic, peeled and whole
2 tablespoons chopped parsley
3½ oz/100 g mussels, cleaned
   (see page 70)
3½ oz/100 g clams, cleaned
   (see page 57)
1¾ oz/50 g onion, thinly sliced
4 tomatoes, peeled and thinly
   sliced (see page 26)
7 oz/200 g musky octopus,
   cleaned and cut into small
   pieces
7 oz/200 g tub gurnard fillets, cut
   into 1-inch/2.5-cm diamonds
3½ oz/100 g red mullet fillets, cut
   into 1-inch/2.5-cm diamonds
1¾ oz/50 g squid rings
7 oz/200 g small cuttlefish,
   cleaned (see page 60) and cut
   into small rings
salt, freshly ground black pepper,
   or crumbled dried red chili
   pepper

Heat 1 tablespoon of oil in a pan over medium heat with the garlic clove and 1 tablespoon of parsley for 1–2 minutes. Add the mussels and clams and cook for 4–5 minutes until opened, then discard the shells and strain the cooking liquid before putting to one side.

Heat the remaining oil in a pan with a lid over low heat and gently fry the onion for 5 minutes. When the onion is browned, add the tomatoes. Leave to cook for 5 minutes, then add all the fish fillets, squid rings, and cuttlefish, with salt to taste. Cook for a further 15–20 minutes, adding a few ladlefuls of hot water to the sauce if necessary. Towards the end of the cooking time, add the mussels and clams and their liquid. Then add the orecchiette to the seafood sauce and cook in the broth until al dente.

Serve the orecchiette in the hot seafood sauce, garnished with the remaining parsley and freshly ground black pepper (or crumbled red chili pepper).

ORECCHIETTE, A TALE FROM PUGLIA

In the collective imagination, Puglia is the region of the trulli. But without a doubt, Puglia at mealtimes evokes the pasta shape that is the crown jewel of that land: orecchiette. Along the alleys of the ancient white-stone villages, women still meet to make them by hand, chatting and laughing as they work. There is nothing more iconic and representative than this round, concave pasta shape—smooth on the inside and rough on the outside—to tell the tales of this region of olive trees and, by extension, the pasta culture of Southern Italy.

The name "orecchiette" brings to mind children's ears, small and soft, the shape of which inspired this style of pasta. So where did this shape originate? Some historians say it dates back to the pasta-style crosets of medieval Provence, made with locally produced durum wheat and able to be preserved for a long time. The Angioini are then said to have introduced orecchiette to Southern Italy in the thirteenth century, when they arrived there after leaving Provence. In the archives of the Basilica di San Nicola in Bari, a sixteenth-century notary deed was found in which the owner of a bakery left his shop to his daughter, mentioning in the marriage dowry the art of preparing the famous 'recchjetedde'.

Yet another story involves Bari's Jewish community during the Norman Svevo dominion, and indicates that Bari orecchiette were inspired by a typical Jewish sweet, Aman's ears. A popular idea, however, is that the shape of orecchiette somehow reflects the rounded shape of the stone roofs of the trulli. The true origins, as is often the case, lie somewhere between history and legend. What is certain is that orecchiette found their motherland in Puglia, becoming an integral part of the region's very identity.

ARTISAN PRODUCTION

Orecchiette are made with a dough of durum wheat semolina and warm water. The mixture is left to rest and then rolled into strings about the width of a little finger, which are cut into cylinders. The final step calls for great manual agility, with fingers dancing between the "*sferre*"—the typical handle-less knife with rounded point—and the dough, which is dragged on the work surface and curled around the finger, so the external surface of the pasta is rough. Easier said than done! You need patience and practice to achieve the correct levels of dexterity.

But this is an art, passed down through the generations, from watching the swift hands of mammas and nonnas.

SAUCES AND FUN FACTS

Today, Pugliesi orecchiette are known and eaten all over the world. The reason behind their success? Maybe it's due to that rough surface and smooth concave shape that allows them to pair well with lots of different sauces and ingredients, from the more traditional meat ragùs to the famous cime di rapa (broccoli rabe). If you happen to travel through Puglia, keep in mind that—as is the case throughout Italy—each town and village has its own variation on the traditional recipes.

In fact, orecchiette are such a complete part of Puglian life that in the past they were even used to predict the gender of unborn children. A mother-to-be would throw one orecchietta and one piece of a long pasta shape known as zito into some boiling water. If the orecchietta floated first, it indicated a baby girl; if the zito rose to the surface, it would be a boy.

CANNELLONI WITH ASPARAGUS AND DRIED CODFISH

50 min   45 min

SERVES 4

12 cannelloni

FOR THE BÉCHAMEL
1¾ tablespoons (1 oz/25 g) butter
¼ cup (¾ oz/20 g) all-purpose
  (plain) flour
2 cups (17 floz/500 ml) milk,
  boiling
salt

FOR THE SAUCE
2¾ tablespoons extra virgin olive
  oil
1 oz/30 g shallot, chopped
1 clove garlic, peeled and whole
14 oz/400 g asparagus, cut into
  thin rounds
8¾ oz/250 g salted codfish,
  soaked in water for 24 hours
  and cut into pieces
4 tablespoons vegetable broth
  (stock)
1 oz/30 g Parmigiano Reggiano,
  grated
salt and freshly ground black
  pepper

For the béchamel, melt the butter in a pan over low heat, add the flour, and leave to cook for 3–4 minutes, stirring constantly with a whisk. Gradually add the boiling milk and salt to taste, and continue cooking, stirring constantly to avoid clumps, until you get a thick, creamy sauce.

For the sauce, heat the oil in a pan over medium heat and fry the shallot and garlic clove for 2–3 minutes, then add the asparagus and cook for another few minutes until browned. Add the codfish, adjust the salt and pepper to taste, then pour in the broth (stock) and bring to a simmer. Cook for 10 minutes, then leave to cool and blend using an immersion blender.

Preheat the oven to 350°F (180°C/Gas Mark 4).

Fill the cannelloni with the fish mixture, then place in a greased baking dish and cover with the béchamel. Sprinkle over the grated Parmigiano.

Cover with foil and cook in the oven for 10 minutes, then remove the foil and cook for a further 10 minutes. Leave the cannelloni to rest for 5 minutes before serving.

Tip
For the perfect béchamel, leave to simmer very gently for at least 30 minutes to allow the flour to lose its flavor and take on the sweetness of the milk.

CASARECCE WITH ANCHOVY AND WILD FENNEL

25 min   12 min

SERVES 4

12 oz/350 g casarecce or bronze-
    drawn linguine
3 tablespoons extra virgin olive oil,
    plus extra for drizzling
4 tablespoons fresh bread crumbs
1 clove garlic, peeled and whole
5¼ oz/150 g anchovies, deboned
2 sprigs wild fennel, chopped
generous ⅛ cup (¾ oz/20 g) pine
    nuts
⅛ cup (¾ oz/20 g) pistachios
scant ¼ cup (1½ oz/40 g) dried
    apricots, cut into strips
1 oz/30 g parsley, chopped
salt and freshly ground black
    pepper

Heat 1 tablespoon oil in a nonstick pan and toast the bread crumbs for 2–3 minutes until crispy. Put to one side.

Heat the remaining oil in a wide pan on medium heat with the garlic clove for 1–2 minutes. Add the anchovies and continue cooking for another 1–2 minutes, then stir in the wild fennel, pine nuts, pistachios, and apricots, and after 30 seconds remove from the heat. Discard the garlic clove, adjust salt and pepper to taste, and put the sauce to one side.

In the meantime, cook the pasta in plenty of salted, boiling water according to the packet instructions. Drain when al dente, and transfer to the pan with the sauce and cook for another couple of minutes. Drizzle over a little oil, the toasted bread crumbs, and parsley and serve.

Tip
Wild fennel is not always easy to find, so it can be substituted with green fronds of fennel, a part of the vegetable that is normally thrown away despite being an excellent flavoring for many dishes, especially fish.

BUCATINI WITH MUSSELS

30 min   12 min

SERVES 4

11 oz/320 g bucatini or linguine
4 tablespoons extra virgin olive oil
1 clove garlic, peeled and whole
1 fresh red chili pepper, chopped
¾ oz/20 g parsley, chopped
28¼ oz/800 g mussels, cleaned
   (see page 70)
1 lb 2 oz/500 g tomatoes, peeled
   and chopped (see page 26)
5 basil leaves, ripped
salt and freshly ground black
   pepper

Heat the oil in a pan on low heat and gently brown the garlic clove, chili pepper, and parsley for 1–2 minutes. Add the mussels and cook until open, about 3–4 minutes, then strain the cooking liquid and discard most of the shells.

Add the chopped tomatoes to the mussels, with salt and pepper to taste, and cook for 2 minutes, then keep warm off the heat.

In the meantime, cook the pasta in plenty of salted, boiling water according to the packet instructions. Drain when al dente, and add to the pan of mussels with the basil, cooking everything together for 2 minutes before serving.

BUCATINI WITH EGGPLANT AND SWORDFISH

30 min   15 min

SERVES 4

11 oz/320 g bucatini or orecchiette
scant 1 cup (7 fl oz/200 ml)
    vegetable oil
7 oz/200 g eggplant (aubergine),
    diced
generous ¾ cup (7 fl oz/200 ml)
    extra virgin olive oil
1 clove garlic, chopped
7 oz/200 g swordfish, diced
5¼ oz/150 g cherry tomatoes,
    cut into wedges
⅓ cup (3 fl oz/80 ml) white wine
8 basil leaves
salt and freshly ground black
    pepper

Heat the vegetable oil in a pan over high heat and, once hot, add the eggplant (aubergines) and fry for 3–4 minutes, spooning them onto kitchen paper with a fish slice when golden.

Heat the extra virgin olive oil in a pan over medium heat, then add the garlic for 1–2 minutes until browned. Add the fish, turning for a few minutes until golden on each side.

Add the cherry tomatoes, stirring and cooking for a couple of minutes, then pour in the wine, leaving it to cook until totally evaporated. Adjust salt and pepper to taste, rip 6 of the basil leaves with your fingers, and sprinkle over the sauce, then remove from the heat.

In the meantime, cook the pasta in plenty of salted, boiling water according to the packet instructions. Drain when al dente, combine with the sauce, fried eggplant, the remaining basil leaves, and serve.

ZUCCHINI FLOWERS

Zucchini flowers—the blossoms of *Cucurbita pepo*—are well known and widely used in cooking. Typical of spring and summer, they are the most famous edible flowers of Mediterranean cuisine. Their freshness can be gauged by their bright yellow color with orange streaks, and they are sold still attached to zucchini, or removed and gathered in bunches.

The flowers have a very light, delicate flavor, and are ideal with pasta dishes, soups, omelets, and seafood. They are also excellent fried in batter, stuffed and baked, and on pizza. A real temptation for the palate and pleasure for the eye, they are very popular with chefs, lending a pop of color to seasonal menus.

ORECCHIETTE WITH SAUSAGE AND ZUCCHINI FLOWERS

25 min   15 min

SERVES 4

11 oz/320 g orecchiette or egg
   tagliatelle
7 oz/200 g sausages
4 tablespoons extra virgin olive oil
3 tablespoons plus 1½ teaspoons
   heavy (double) cream
chopped parsley
3½ oz/100 g zucchini (courgette)
   flowers
salt and freshly ground black
   pepper

Remove the skins from the sausages and break up the sausage meat. Heat 2 tablespoons of oil in a pan over medium heat, and brown the sausage meat for 3–4 minutes, then add the cream and parsley, season to taste, and cook for 5 minutes.

Cut the zucchini (courgette) flowers lengthwise, and sauté in a pan with the remaining oil on high heat for 3 minutes, turning continually.

Cook the pasta in plenty of salted, boiling water according to the packet instructions. Drain when al dente, combine with the sausage and zucchini flowers, and serve.

GREEN LASAGNE ALLA BOLOGNESE

2 hours   1 hour

SERVES 4

8 sheets of green lasagne
    or egg lasagne

FOR THE RAGÙ
2 tablespoons extra virgin olive oil
5¼ oz/150 g soffritto mix (finely
    diced celery stalk, carrot, and
    onion)
1 bay leaf
3½ oz/100 g ground (minced) pork
4¼ oz/120 g ground (minced) beef
¾ oz/20 g pancetta, chopped
⅓ cup (3 fl oz/80 ml) red wine
2 oz/60 g tomato paste (purée)
salt and freshly ground
    black pepper

FOR THE BÉCHAMEL
2 tablespoons (1 oz/30 g) butter
⅕ cup (¾ oz/25 g) all-purpose
    (plain) flour
2 cups (17 fl oz/500 ml) milk,
    boiling
whole nutmeg, for grating

FOR THE GARNISH
2¾ oz/80 g Parmigiano Reggiano,
    grated
1 tablespoon plus 1 teaspoon
    (¾ oz/20 g) butter

For the ragù, heat the oil in a pan over medium heat and brown the soffritto mix with the bay leaf for 2–3 minutes. When browned, add the ground (minced) meats and the pancetta, and turn up the heat to brown. As soon as the meat changes color, add salt and pepper to taste, and pour in the red wine. Leave to evaporate completely.

Turn down the heat to low and add the tomato paste (purée). Add enough water to just cover, and cook gently for 1 hour.

For the béchamel, melt the butter in a pan over low heat, add the flour, and leave to cook for 3–4 minutes, stirring constantly with a whisk. Gradually add the boiling milk, salt, and a grating of nutmeg and continue cooking, stirring constantly to avoid clumps, until you get a thick, creamy sauce.

Preheat the oven to 340°F (170°C/Gas Mark 3).

Grease a baking dish and spread with a layer of lasagne sheets. Then spoon an even layer of ragù on top, then the béchamel, and a generous handful of Parmigiano. Continue this until you have used up all the ingredients. Finish with a layer of béchamel and a generous sprinkling of cheese, then add a few flakes of butter.

Cook the lasagne for 20 minutes until bubbling and golden brown, then leave to rest for 5 minutes before serving.

EGG FETTUCCINE ALLA BOLOGNESE

25 min   2 hours

SERVES 4

8¾ oz/250 g egg fettuccine
   or egg tagliatelle
⅓ cup plus 1 tablespoon (3½ fl
   oz/100 ml) extra virgin olive oil
4¼ oz/120 g soffritto mix (finely
   diced celery stalk, carrot,
   and onion)
2 bay leaves
5¼ oz/150 g minced pork lard
5¼ oz/150 g pork shoulder,
   chopped
5¼ oz/150 g lean beef, chopped
⅓ cup plus 1 tablespoon
   (3½ fl oz/100 ml) red wine
3¼ oz/90 g tomato paste (purée)
1½ oz/40 g Parmigiano Reggiano,
   grated
salt and freshly ground black
   pepper

Heat the oil in a pan over a medium heat and brown the
soffritto mix with the bay leaves and lard for 2–3 minutes.
Add the meats and increase the heat so it browns well. Add
the red wine and leave to evaporate for a couple of minutes.

Reduce the heat to low and add the tomato paste (purée).
Add salt and pepper to taste and pour in a little water
to loosen the sauce. Leave to simmer for around 2 hours.

In the meantime, cook the pasta in plenty of salted, boiling
water according to the packet instructions. Drain when
al dente and stir through the ragù. Serve with a sprinkling
of Parmigiano.

EGG PAPPARDELLE WITH LAMB AND ARTICHOKE RAGÙ

30 min   30 min

SERVES 4

8¾ oz/250 g egg pappardelle or
    paglia e fieno
4 tablespoons extra virgin olive oil
1 onion, chopped
1 clove garlic, chopped
1 sprig rosemary
1 sprig thyme
1 bay leaf
10½ oz/300 g lean lamb meat,
    diced
⅓ cup plus 1 tablespoon (3½ fl
    oz/100 ml) dry white wine
3½ oz/100 g canned crushed
    tomatoes
⅓ cup plus 1 tablespoon
    (3½ fl oz/100 ml) vegetable or
    meat broth (stock) (optional)
4 artichokes, cleaned and cut into
    strips
2¾ oz/80 g Pecorino Romano,
    grated or shaved
salt and freshly ground black
    pepper

Heat half of the oil in a pan and cook the onion with the garlic, rosemary, thyme, and bay leaf for 5 minutes until browned.

Add the lamb and brown all over, about 5 minutes. Add salt and pepper to taste, and pour in the white wine. Cook until the wine has evaporated completely, 3–4 minutes, then add the crushed tomatoes and cook for around 15 minutes, adding broth (stock) if necessary.

In the meantime, heat the remaining oil in another pan and sauté the artichokes with a little salt for 5 minutes. Add to the lamb when there is 5 minutes of the cooking time left.

Cook the pasta in plenty of salted, boiling water according to the packet instructions. Drain when al dente and combine with the sauce. Serve sprinkled with Pecorino.

LIVING WELL

LIVING WELL

A STORY OF GOOD LIVING

"There is no place in the world that I love more than the kitchen." This is how Banana Yoshimoto opens *Kitchen*, the Japanese author's first novel, published in Italy in the world's first translation in 1991. There are certainly many Italians who remember doing their school homework in the family kitchen, sitting at the same table on which they had just enjoyed lunch with their family, and perhaps with some friends as guests. And it is in kitchens, observing those who move with ease between ingredients and stoves, experimenting with old and new recipes, that you ultimately learn elements of history, geography, biology, chemistry, and even poetry. In kitchens, our desires intersect, and emotions and feelings become an integral part of the recipes.

The kitchen is also where changes linked to new lifestyles and new dietary needs manifest themselves: eating well—a synthesis between the goodness of taste and the lightness of body and soul—is a choice that nourishes one's overall well-being and implies an awareness of the origin of the ingredients and a certain familiarity with the nutritional properties of foods. It means getting in tune with food through the five senses and, therefore, eating unhurriedly, evaluating the aromas, sounds, textures, and colors the dishes have to offer, allowing ourselves to appreciate the sensations that are generated in the mind and body. The cult of good food, and of beauty in general—for which the Italians are famous—combined with the extraordinary biodiversity that characterizes the country, perhaps makes it easier for them to truly live the "good life." Perhaps it is in their DNA.

In this context, pasta becomes the medium, the glue between different needs and lifestyles, a food genuinely capable of adapting and evolving. Barilla therefore offers the possibility of choosing pasta with a different composition to the classic semolina variety, with a range of whole grain (wholemeal) and gluten free pastas, as well as those made from legumes and other cereals. They are products created in response to new market needs and widespread sensitivities that have emerged in recent years, including new food ethics, the rediscovery of noninvasive agriculture, biological conversions of land, and the valorization of gastronomic biodiversity. Legumes have become a full member of the pasta family, with pastas made with chickpeas, red lentils, peas, or sometimes even bean flours, just as pasta shapes prepared with a mix of legume and grain flours, such as corn and rice, are now readily available. Pasta has been given a new look, taking on new textures and, thanks to its more distinctly protein composition, allowing for a more intense dialogue with vegetables. All without sacrificing taste.

SUSTAINABLE CHOICES IN THE KITCHEN

In 2010, the Mediterranean Diet was officially designated an "Intangible Cultural Heritage" by UNESCO, recognizing the union between gastronomic pleasure and good living. It is identity and belonging, a perfect balance between nature and knowledge, which also encompasses a new understanding of the relationship between territory, raw materials, and sustainability. From the ground to the finished dish, here is the best path to approach a balanced lifestyle in tune with the environment, discovering and experimenting with new types of pasta in the kitchen.

The recipes that follow will surprise you with their creativity and simplicity, their ability to respond to different dietary needs, uniting awareness with flavor. They are recipes accessible to all, designed so that everyone can find their own dimension of good living.

RED LENTIL PENNE WITH VEGETABLES

40 min 20 min

SERVES 4

11 oz/320 g red lentil penne or
  whole grain (wholemeal)
  casarecce
3 tablespoons plus 1½ teaspoons
  extra virgin olive oil
1¾ oz/50 g leeks, sliced
1¾ oz/50 g carrot, cubed
1¾ oz/50 g celery stalk, cubed
2 oz/60 g pumpkin flesh, cubed
1¾ oz/50 g eggplant (aubergine),
  cubed
1¾ oz/50 g zucchini (courgette),
  cubed
1¾ oz/50 g red bell pepper,
  deseeded and diced
1¾ oz/50 g yellow bell pepper,
  deseeded and diced
1 oz/25 g shelled peas
2 oz/60 g tomato, cubed
6 basil leaves, coarsely chopped
salt

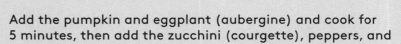

Heat the oil in a pan, and cook the leeks, carrot, and celery
for 3–4 minutes until browned.

Add the pumpkin and eggplant (aubergine) and cook for
5 minutes, then add the zucchini (courgette), peppers, and
peas, with 5–6 tablespoons of hot water if needed. Season
with salt to taste and cook for 5 minutes.

Add the tomatoes and continue cooking for 5 minutes, then
stir through the basil.

While the ragù is cooking, cook the pasta in plenty of
salted, boiling water according to the packet instructions.
Drain the pasta when al dente, top with the ragù, and serve.

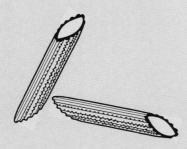

WHOLE GRAIN PENNE RIGATE MEDITERRANEAN SALAD

20 min   8 min

SERVES 4

12¼ oz/350 g whole grain
   (wholemeal) penne rigate or
   casarecce
⅓ cup (3 fl oz/80 ml) extra virgin
   olive oil
1¾ oz/50 g shelled peas
3½ oz/100 g shelled fava (broad)
   beans
2 tablespoons capers
scant ⅓ cup (1¾ oz/50 g) black
   olives, pitted
7 oz/200 g San Marzano
   tomatoes, chopped
2¾ oz/80 g red bell pepper,
   deseeded and diced
2¾ oz/80 g yellow bell pepper,
   deseeded and diced
2¾ oz/80 g cucumber, deseeded
   and diced
1¾ oz/50 g celery stalk, diced
1½ oz/40 g Tropea onion, sliced
dried oregano, to serve
salt

Cook the pasta in plenty of salted, boiling water according to the packet instructions. Drain while still very al dente, and cool by running it briefly under cold running water. Pour into a serving bowl and drizzle with a little of the oil to prevent it from sticking.

In the meantime, blanch the peas for 1 minute in salted, boiling water, then cool immediately in iced water. Do the same with the fava (broad) beans, then remove their skins.

Rinse the capers and olives to remove any brine, then mix all the ingredients together with the cooked pasta. Finish with a pinch of salt, the remaining oil, and a sprinkling of oregano, and serve.

Tip
This recipe is perfect with short pasta. You can substitute the penne rigate or casarecce with cellentani, farfalle, and fusilli (whole grain/wholemeal or otherwise).

WHOLE GRAIN PENNE GRATIN WITH SCALLIONS AND BEETS

The piquant aroma of the scallions (spring onions) contrasts boldly with the sweet fragrance of the beets (beetroot) and combines beautifully with the béchamel sauce before you dive into the freshly cooked penne. A recipe that is crunchy on the top and soft in the center.

40 min   25 min

SERVES 4

11 oz/320 g whole grain (wholemeal) penne or casarecce
2 tablespoons extra virgin olive oil
1 scallion (spring onion), sliced
7 oz/200 g cooked beets (beetroot), cubed
grated Parmigiano Reggiano, for dusting
salt

FOR THE BÉCHAMEL
1¾ tablespoons (1 oz/25 g) butter
2 cups (17 fl oz/500 ml) milk, boiling
⅕ cup (1 oz/25 g) all-purpose (plain) flour
pinch of grated nutmeg
salt

For the béchamel, melt the butter in a pan over low heat, add the flour, and leave to cook for 3–4 minutes, stirring constantly with a whisk. Gradually add the boiling milk, salt, and a grating of nutmeg and continue cooking, stirring constantly to avoid clumps, until you get a thick, creamy sauce.

In the meantime, heat the oil in a skillet (frying pan) and cook the scallion (spring onion) and beets (beetroot) for 3–4 minutes. In a food processor or blender, blend everything to a purée, then stir the purée through the bechamel.

Preheat the oven to 400°F (200°C/Gas Mark 6).

Cook the pasta in plenty of salted, boiling water according to the packet instructions. Drain when al dente, then stir through the sauce. Pour it into a baking dish, dust with a little grated Parmigiano, and leave to cook for 5–10 minutes until a light crust forms.

Tip
All gratin dishes can also be served as single portions: divide the pasta into single portion casserole dishes and cook as described.

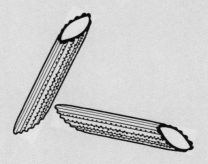

WHOLE GRAIN PENNETTE WITH LEMON-SCENTED VEGETABLE PESTO

In the Campo de' Fiori market in Rome, artichokes and asparagus are often found close together: not a natural combination to begin with, but friends soon enough. Cook them carefully alongside the whole grain (wholemeal) pennette and scent everything with lemon. *La dolce vita.*

30 min   20 min

SERVES 4

11 oz/320 g whole grain (wholemeal) pennette or legume casarecce
1 cup (8½ fl oz/250 ml) milk
2¾ oz/80 g Taleggio (or similar cheese), cut into small pieces
1¾ tablespoons extra virgin olive oil
1 clove garlic, peeled and whole
10½ oz/300 g artichoke stalks (peeled and cut into pieces) and asparagus stalks (peeled)
grated zest of 1 unwaxed lemon
salt and freshly ground black pepper

In a pan over low heat, warm the milk, then add the cheese and stir until melted.

Heat the oil in a pan over medium heat with the garlic clove for 2 minutes, then sauté the vegetables for 3–4 minutes; add a little hot water, if needed, to aid the cooking process. Discard the garlic clove, pour in the Taleggio milk, and put to one side.

Cook the pasta in plenty of salted, boiling water according to the packet instructions. Drain when al dente, and pour into the pan, mixing everything together with a wooden spoon. Add the grated lemon zest and serve.

Tip
All vegetable leftovers have unlimited potential. Set aside (or freeze) any waste parts for use in a vegetable broth.

LEMON

The lemon, *Citrus limonum*, is the fruit of a small evergreen tree. It is an essential ingredient of Mediterranean cuisine, known and appreciated for its fresh, vibrant citrus flavor. Originally from Asia, cultivation spread to Italy in the mid-fifteenth century, especially in the south of the peninsula or in areas with a mild climate even during the coldest seasons.

It is a versatile ingredient, used in many savory dishes thanks to its acidity, which allows it to balance flavors. Lemon juice is often used in meat and fish dishes, salads, and drinks, and added to sauces and marinades—it can comple-tely transform a dish, giving it a citrus and aromatic note.

Some well-known pasta dishes that include lemon are pasta al limone and spaghetti with sea urchins and lemon, while it also pairs well with mullet and chicken. A sprinkling of finely grated zest over a dish gives it a lift and an aroma of freshness.

RED LENTIL SPAGHETTI WITH VEGETABLE PESTO

30 min   15 min

SERVES 4

11 oz/320 g red lentil spaghetti or
    gluten free spaghetti
1 carrot, chopped
1 leek, chopped
1 whole fennel bulb (keep the
    fronds to one side), chopped
1¾ oz/50 g shelled peas
3 celery stalks, chopped,
    plus 1¾ oz/50 g celery leaves
1¾ oz/50 g Parmigiano Reggiano,
    grated
¾ cup (1¾ oz/50 g) blanched
    almonds
1 clove garlic (optional)
⅓ cup (3½ fl oz/100 ml) almond
    milk (sugar free)
3 tablespoons plus 1½ teaspoons
    extra virgin olive oil
grated zest of ½ unwaxed lemon
3 tablespoons slivered almonds
salt and freshly ground black
    pepper

Blanch the vegetables together in lightly salted boiling water for a few minutes. Cool them all in iced water, setting the cooking water to one side for the pasta.

Transfer the drained vegetables to a blender with the Parmigiano, blanched almonds, garlic (if using), and salt and pepper to taste, and, gradually, add the almond milk. Finally, add 2 tablespoons of oil and the grated lemon zest.

Cook the pasta in plenty of salted, boiling water for three-quarters of the time indicated in the packet instructions, then drain—reserving a little of the cooking water—and transfer to the pan with the pesto to continue cooking for 5 minutes. If necessary, add a little pasta cooking water to loosen.

Place the pasta in a serving dish and top with the slivered almonds, a few fennel fronds, and the remaining olive oil.

WHOLE GRAIN SPAGHETTI WITH FENNEL AND TOMATO PESTO

The strands of whole grain (wholemeal) spaghetti unite with the sweet crunchiness of the fennel, the deep flavor of the tomato, and the freshness of the celery. Summer is finally here.

25 min   8 min

SERVES 4

11 oz/320 g whole grain (wholemeal) spaghetti or legume spaghetti
10½ oz/300 g fennel bulb, chopped
1 small bunch basil
1 handful of celery leaves
4 tablespoons extra virgin olive oil
juice of ½ lemon
2 oz/60 g Parmigiano Reggiano, grated
3 vine tomatoes, diced
salt and freshly ground black pepper

For the pesto, blanch the fennel for 1 minute in a pan of salted, boiling water. Drain, and leave to cool.

Once cooled, put the fennel in a blender with a pinch of salt, the fresh basil, most of the celery leaves, the oil, and a few drops of lemon juice. Blend well, adding the grated Parmigiano to incorporate. Adjust salt and pepper to taste.

Cook the pasta in plenty of salted, boiling water according to the packet instructions. Drain when al dente—reserving a little of the cooking water—and stir through the fennel pesto. If necessary, add a little of the cooking water to make the pesto more liquid. Top with the diced tomato and garnish with the remaining celery leaves.

Tips
For a colorful, sustainable garnish, blanch a ripe red tomato for a few minutes in a pan of salted, boiling water, then peel off four slices of skin. Place them on a parchment-lined sheet pan (baking tray) and leave to dry for 1 hour in an oven at 210°F (100°C/Gas Mark ¼).

To give more crunch to the dish, garnish it with thin slivers of toasted almonds.

WHOLE GRAIN SPAGHETTI WITH OIL, PEPPER, AND PARMIGIANO

Rich in starch and salts, cooking water is ideal for helping to blend pasta and sauce. It is able to create that wonderful cream, which—together with oil and black pepper—lends softness and flavor to the sauce. This is a simple but unforgettable spaghetti dish.

10 min   8 min

SERVES 4

11 oz/320 g whole grain (wholemeal) spaghetti or gluten free spaghetti
5 tablespoons plus 1½ teaspoons extra virgin olive oil
3½ oz/100 g aged Parmigiano Reggiano, grated
salt and freshly ground black pepper

Cook the pasta in plenty of salted, boiling water according to the packet instructions. Drain when al dente, reserving a little of the cooking water.

Transfer the pasta to a serving bowl and add the oil, two-thirds of the Parmigiano and ⅓ cup (3½ fl oz/100 ml) of the cooking water.

Serve immediately with the remaining Parmigiano and a generous grinding of black pepper.

Tip
If desired, add a dusting of fresh aromatic herbs (lemon thyme, chives, parsley) to each plate before serving.

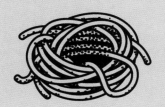

WHOLE GRAIN SPAGHETTI WITH CRUNCHY VEGETABLES AND ALMONDS

25 min   15 min

SERVES 4

11 oz/320 g whole grain
    (wholemeal) spaghetti or
    gluten free spaghetti
3 tablespoons plus 1½ teaspoons
    extra virgin olive oil, plus extra
    for drizzling
1¾ oz/50 g leeks, julienned
5¼ oz/150 g zucchini (courgettes),
    julienned
5¼ oz/150 g red bell pepper,
    julienned
5¼ oz/150 g yellow bell pepper,
    julienned
3½ oz/100 g carrot, julienned
1¾ oz/50 g celery stalk, sliced
1¼ oz/35 g shallot, finely chopped
10 basil leaves, coarsely chopped
3 tablespoons slivered almonds
salt and freshly ground black
    pepper

Heat the oil in a pan over medium heat and brown the vegetables for 3–4 minutes; they should still be crunchy. Adjust salt to taste, and add half of the basil.

Cook the pasta in plenty of salted, boiling water according to the packet instructions, then drain when al dente, reserving a little of the cooking water.

Transfer the pasta to a serving bowl and combine with the vegetables and slivered almonds, adding a few tablespoons of the pasta cooking water to loosen, if needed. Complete with a drizzle of oil, the remaining basil leaves, and freshly ground pepper.

PASTA

NOT JUST SEMOLINA

Until recently, "alternative" pastas such as legume and whole grain (wholemeal) were either not widely available, or considered a dietary sacrifice for health, while gluten free pasta was seen as purely a resource for those with celiac disease or who are gluten intolerant but don't want to forego their pasta dishes. Increasingly, these new pastas represent an exciting evolution in the world of nutrition, combining taste and wellbeing without neglecting gourmet principles, and appealing to all.

WHOLE GRAIN PASTA

Whole grain (wholemeal) pasta is obtained using a different wheat processing process; in traditional semolina pasta the bran part of the wheat grain is eliminated, whereas in whole grain pasta the semolina also contains the external parts of the grain, made up mainly of vegetable fibers, mineral salts, and group B vitamins. Indeed, scientific studies show that regular consumption of whole grain products may help to reduce the risk of cardiovascular disease. Whole grain pasta is slightly darker in color due to the presence of bran and has a stronger flavor than "regular" pasta. It is important to choose a durum wheat with a good protein content so as to ensure the correct texture of the pasta.

GLUTEN FREE PASTA

Today, gluten free pasta is widely available, and can be easily sourced in most shops. It is made with a mix of flours such as rice flour, corn or millet, or quinoa and soy. When processed correctly, these blends play a structural role; by not using traditional durum wheat semolina, pasta technologists create an "alternative scaffold" to gluten, which gives structure to the final product. Without this sort of internal structure, the pasta would not maintain its typical al dente consistency after cooking in water. The ingredients and unique production process also contribute to improving the sensorial characteristics of the pasta.

From a nutritional point of view, gluten free pasta does not differ much from traditional durum wheat semolina pasta in terms of carbohydrates and fiber. It does, however, contain less protein. Gluten free pasta —particularly that made with rice or corn flour—contains a higher quantity of vitamin B3 than semolina pasta, and slightly higher quantities of calcium, phosphorus, magnesium, potassium, sodium, and iron in terms of mineral salts. On a caloric level, there are no substantial differences.

LEGUME PASTA

Have you ever tried red lentil spaghetti with celery pesto? Or a plate of green pea fusilli? Legume pasta is innovative, versatile, and much-loved by all those looking for a varied and healthy lifestyle. Naturally gluten free and rich in protein and fiber, it represents one of the new international food trends and has experienced significant growth in recent years. Popular legumes include red lentils, chickpeas, green peas, and black beans, offering a wide range of potential colors and flavors.

This pasta, which cooks quickly and has a uniform consistency, holds up very well when cooked. The color-flavor correlation of the pasta, linked to the type of legumes used, offers an aromatic and sensory experience, allowing ample opportunity to explore new combinations of accompanying ingredients to create a variety of innovative and exciting dishes.

In conclusion, legume, whole grain (wholemeal), and gluten free pastas provide new opportunities to satisfy various dietary needs and support a healthy lifestyle without giving up the taste and imagination that have always accompanied the versatility of pasta.

GLUTEN FREE SPAGHETTI WITH CITRUS PESTO

15 min   10 min

SERVES 4

11 oz/320 g gluten free spaghetti
    or whole grain (wholemeal)
    spaghetti
2 oz/60 g arugula (rocket), plus
    extra to garnish
⅓ cup (2 oz/50 g) almonds
2 oranges, peel and pith removed
1 lemon, peel and pith removed
1 oz/30 g Parmigiano Reggiano,
    grated
1 oz/30 g Pecorino Romano,
    grated
extra virgin olive oil
salt

Place the arugula (rocket) in a blender with the almonds, half the lemon, 1 orange, Parmigiano, and Pecorino, and start to blend. Drizzle in as much oil as needed until you get a smooth, bright pesto.

Cut the remaining lemon and orange into small cubes and set to one side.

In the meantime, cook the pasta in plenty of salted, boiling water according to the packet instructions, and drain when al dente. Combine with the pesto and garnish with the arugula leaves and cubes of fruit.

GLUTEN FREE PENNE RIGATE WITH CREAM OF CAULIFLOWER, PINE NUTS, AND GOLDEN RAISINS

15 min   20 min

SERVES 4

11 oz/320 g gluten free penne
   rigate or whole grain
   (wholemeal) penne
2¾ tablespoons extra virgin
   olive oil
2 sprigs rosemary, plus extra
   leaves, to garnish
2 oz/50 g soft gluten free bread,
   ripped into pieces
¼ cup (1½ oz/40 g) golden raisins
   (sultanas), soaked and chopped
⅓ cup (1½ oz/40 g) pine nuts
1 clove garlic, peeled and whole
14 oz/400 g cauliflower stalks and
   florets, cut into pieces
8 anchovy fillets
salt and freshly ground black
   pepper

Heat 1 tablespoon of oil with a sprig of rosemary in a nonstick skillet (frying pan) over medium heat and toast the soft bread. Add the golden raisins (sultanas) and pine nuts, remove the rosemary, then set the contents of the pan aside.

In the same pan, heat the remaining oil and rosemary sprig, and the garlic clove. Leave for a moment for the flavors to infuse, then add the cauliflower and a ladleful of boiling water. Cook for a few minutes to soften the cauliflower, then add the anchovy fillets and, once broken up, adjust salt and pepper to taste. Transfer to a blender and blend to a sauce consistency.

Cook the pasta in plenty of salted, boiling water according to the packet instructions. Drain when al dente, and pour into the pan with the creamed cauliflower. Garnish with the bread, golden raisin and pine nut topping, and a few rosemary leaves.

GLUTEN FREE TORTIGLIONI WITH ZUCCHINI CARBONARA

10 min   10 min

SERVES 4

11 oz/320 g gluten free tortiglioni
   or gluten free penne rigate
4 egg yolks
3½ oz/100 g Pecorino Romano,
   grated
1 tablespoon plus 1 teaspoon milk
2 tablespoons extra virgin olive oil
5 oz/140 g zucchini (courgettes),
   julienned
salt and freshly ground black
   pepper

In a mixing bowl, beat the egg yolks with a pinch of salt, one-third of the grated Pecorino cheese, and the milk.

Heat the oil in a skillet (frying pan) over medium heat and, when hot, add the zucchini (courgettes), and cook for 2–3 minutes, until browned but still crunchy.

In the meantime, cook the pasta in plenty of salted, boiling water according to the packet instructions. Drain the pasta when al dente, reserving a little of the cooking water. Add the pasta to the pan with the zucchini, mix well, turn off the heat, and pour in the beaten eggs, adding 2 tablespoons of the cooking water. Mix for around 30 seconds, add the rest of the Pecorino, mix again, and serve with a generous grinding of black pepper.

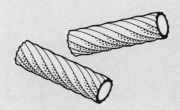

WHOLE GRAIN PENNE WITH ASPARAGUS CREAM

Delicate and refined, yet thick and soft, the asparagus crème is a simple condiment that is the perfect partner to the exuberant whole grain (wholemeal) penne. A dish that feels a lot like springtime.

30 min   20 min

SERVES 4

11 oz/320 g whole grain (wholemeal) penne or legume spaghetti
1 tablespoon plus 1 teaspoon extra virgin olive oil
1 oz/30 g shallot, sliced
1 lb/450 g asparagus, cleaned and cut into rounds, reserving the tips
⅓ cup (3½ fl oz/100 ml) heavy (double) cream
3½ oz/100 g Parmigiano Reggiano, grated
salt

Heat the oil in a pan over medium heat and cook the shallot for 5 minutes until lightly browned, then add the asparagus rounds and cook for 2 minutes. Cover with 2 cups (17 fl oz/500 ml) water and cook for 15 minutes. Add a little salt, then blend everything to a creamy sauce using an immersion blender.

Blanch the asparagus tips in a separate pan of salted, boiling water for 3–4 minutes, then cool immediately in iced water.

Cook the pasta in plenty of salted, boiling water according to the packet instructions. Drain when al dente, and pour into the pan of sauce, adding the asparagus tips, cream, and grated Parmigiano. Mix everything over heat for 1 minute before serving.

Tip
For a lighter version, omit the cream or substitute with plant-based cream.

WHOLE GRAIN CASARECCE WITH TOMATOES AND OLIVES

Nature provides them in small vines, with a bright red color and sweet flavor. When paired with Taggiasca olives and basil oil, cherry tomatoes give us a sauce that is also a journey: from Campania to Liguria, it's all of Italy in a single dish.

20 min   10 min

SERVES 4

14 oz/400 g whole grain (wholemeal) casarecce or gluten free spaghetti
4 tablespoons extra virgin olive oil
1 clove garlic, sliced
1 small fresh (sliced) or dried (crumbled) red chili pepper
17½ oz/500 g Datterino tomatoes, quartered
scant ⅓ cup (1¾ oz/50 g) pitted Taggiasca olives, halved
¾ oz/20 g basil
salt

Heat half of the oil in a pan over medium heat and cook the garlic and chili pepper for 2 minutes, making sure they don't brown too much.

Increase the heat to high, add the tomatoes, and salt if needed, and continue to cook for around 5 minutes, stirring occasionally. Add the olives and cook for 1 more minute.

In a food processor or blender, blend the basil with the remaining oil and a pinch of salt.

In the meantime, cook the pasta in plenty of salted, boiling water according to the packet instructions. Drain when al dente, and garnish with the sauce and basil oil.

Tip
For extra flavor, add 5¼ oz/150 g fresh tuna, diced and lightly sautéed.

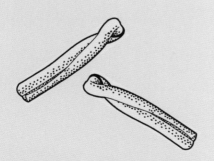

OLIVES

The olive is one of the oldest crops in the world, its history closely intertwined with that of agriculture and food in the Mediterranean basin. Olives come in many different shapes and flavors, depending on location, climate, and cultivation methods. Loved for their taste, they are also appreciated for their health benefits, thanks to their high content of monounsaturated fats and antioxidants.

Taggiasca olives are some of the most famous in the world—small olives with an intense and slightly bitter flavor and a color that varies from dark purple to black, they are used in cooking to enrich appetizers, salads, fish, pizza, and focaccia. The Taggiasca olive arrived in Italy thanks to French monks who settled in Taggia, in western Liguria, between the end of the seventh and the beginning of the eighth century. The microclimatic features of the area have made this product unique and strongly characteristic of the territory.

In addition to Taggiasca, numerous varieties of olives contribute to the diversity and richness of Mediterranean cuisine. The darker the olive, the riper and more intense the flavor—so green olives are more delicate in flavor, while black olives are more robust. There are also pink olives, characteristic of regions such as Puglia, whose particular fermentation process gives them their characteristic color and unique flavor.

LEGUME FUSILLI WITH FAVA BEANS THREE WAYS

Springtime—the time of fava (broad) beans. And when they are cooked in three different ways, the resulting pasta dish cannot be anything but masterly. A dish of great simplicity with genuine flavors from the land.

1 hour   2 hours

SERVES 4

11 oz/320 g legume fusilli or whole grain (wholemeal) fusilli
14 oz/400 g fresh shelled fava (broad) beans (or use frozen)
3 tablespoons plus 1½ teaspoons extra virgin olive oil, plus extra for drizzling
2 shallots, finely chopped
salt and freshly ground black pepper

FOR THE PESTO
1¾ oz/50 g Parmigiano Reggiano, grated
scant ¼ cup (1 oz/30 g) blanched almonds
2¾ tablespoons extra virgin olive oil, plus extra if needed

Blanch the fresh fava (broad) beans in salted, boiling water for around 1 minute (or 2 minutes if you are using frozen fava beans). Remove the skins and divide into three equal amounts.

Preheat the oven to its lowest setting. Place one-third of the fava beans on a parchment-lined sheet pan (baking tray) and leave in the oven for 2 hours to dry.

Heat the oil in a pan over medium heat and lightly sauté another one-third of the beans with the shallots for 3–4 minutes, adding salt and pepper to taste.

For the pesto: in a blender or food processor, blend the remaining beans with the grated Parmigiano, almonds, oil, and a little salt. Should the pesto be too thick, add a little more oil or even a drop of cold water.

Cook the pasta in plenty of salted, boiling water according to the packet instructions. Drain when al dente, and combine with the fava bean pesto. Add the sautéed fava beans, and scatter over the oven-dried beans and a drizzle of oil.

Tips
For the best drying results, do not use the fan oven setting, and leave the door slightly open.

If desired, you could garnish the dish with some thyme flowers or other edible flowers.

LEGUME FUSILLI SALAD WITH MONKFISH AND BEANS

The delicate white flesh of the monkfish contrasts perfectly with the flavors of the beans and olives that the legume fusilli aims to elevate in this dish. Eat it as you look out to the sea.

30 min   15 min

SERVES 4

11 oz/320 g legume fusilli or gluten free penne rigate
⅓ cup (3½ fl oz/100 ml) extra virgin olive oil, plus extra for drizzling and garnishing
1 bunch basil
1 clove garlic, peeled and whole
8¾ oz/250 g monkfish, cut into cubes
vegetable broth (stock) (optional)
7 oz/200 g fresh shelled fava (broad) beans (or use frozen)
scant ⅓ cup (1¾ oz/50 g) black olives
6¼ oz/180 g ripe tomatoes, peeled, deseeded, and diced (see page 26)
salt and freshly ground black pepper

Cook the pasta in plenty of salted, boiling water according to the packet instructions. When still very al dente, remove from the heat and leave to cool slightly, then quickly rinse the pasta under cold running water and leave to drain well. Pour into a large bowl and garnish with a drizzle of oil so it doesn't stick.

Using an immersion blender, blend half the oil with the basil leaves, then strain through a fine sieve.

Heat the remaining oil in a pan over medium heat and fry the clove of garlic for 2 minutes. Add the monkfish, salt and pepper to taste, and cook quickly, for 3 minutes, to avoid the fish flaking. Moisten with a little vegetable broth (stock) if necessary.

Blanch the fresh fava (broad) beans in salted, boiling water for around 1 minute (or 2 minutes if you are using frozen fava beans). Leave to cool, then peel, and season with salt, pepper, and 2 tablespoons of oil. Add the beans, olives, tomatoes, and monkfish to the bowl of pasta and blend together, adjusting salt and pepper to taste. Serve with the basil oil.

Tip
Leave the finished pasta to rest in the fridge for around 2 hours so it better absorbs the flavors and aromas of the sauce. Remember to remove it at least a half-hour before serving, so it is not fridge-cold on the palate.

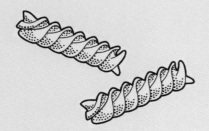

LEGUMOTTI SALAD WITH SHRIMP, PEAS, AND ZUCCHINI

30 min   15 min

SERVES 4

7 oz/200 g legumotti or whole
    grain (wholemeal) penne
6 tablespoons extra virgin
    olive oil
1 red onion, finely chopped
3 carrots, diced
2 zucchini (courgettes), diced
2 oz/50 g peas, shelled and
    blanched (see page 273)
3½ oz/100 g shrimp (prawn) tails
3 vine tomatoes, peeled,
    deseeded, and diced
    (see page 26)
handful of basil leaves, coarsely
    chopped, plus a few extra
    leaves to garnish
salt

Heat 2 tablespoons of oil in a pan over medium heat, add the onion, and cook for 5 minutes until browned. Add the carrots and zucchini (courgettes), with salt to taste, and cook, stirring occasionally, for 2–3 minutes: the vegetables must remain crunchy. Add the blanched peas.

In the meantime, cook the pasta in plenty of salted, boiling water according to the packet instructions, then drain, and add to the vegetables with the diced tomatoes. Combine with the coarsely chopped basil and 2 tablespoons of oil and adjust salt to taste.

Heat the remaining oil in a pan over medium-high heat, and sauté the shrimp (prawn) tails for 3–4 minutes, before adding to the legumotti. Garnish with a few small basil leaves.

THE MEDITERRANEAN DIET

ANCEL KEYS

American doctor and physiologist Ancel Keys was born in Colorado Springs at the beginning of the twentieth century, but his name is forever linked with two places: the Laboratory of Physiological Hygiene, which he founded and directed from 1937 to 1975, and the southern Italian seaside village of Pioppi, in Cilento, Campania, where he lived together with his wife Margareth for over forty years. The Keys bought a house there called "Minnelea," in homage to both the city of Minneapolis and the Magna Graecia polis (ancient Greek state) of Elea, in Cilento, their adopted land.

In the first Italian edition (second English edition) of Keys' book *Eat Well and Stay Well, the Mediterranean Way*, a fundamental text published in 1962, he asks how the everyday diet can achieve a balance between health, wellbeing, and the pleasure of food. For forty years Keys and his colleagues studied—in the field, in one of the most important areas of the Mediterranean— the medical, physiological, cultural, and social aspects linked to the Mediterranean diet, discovering that good health is the result of an active lifestyle and a healthy diet, with simple dishes based on vegetables, legumes, home-made pasta, fish, and extra virgin olive oil. In his studies and in countless scientific publications, Keys points out a recurring fact: while it may be the ingredients that make a difference to the lives of the population, human behaviors, a healthy environment, and the symbiosis between the natural world and culture are also important aspects.

From his observatory in Cilento, Keys studied the inhabitants' daily lives—their work in the fields, fishing at sea, rest time, and their nutritional habits. He captured the sense of sacredness attributed to food, traditions and lifestyles, the sense of parsimony, and, above all, the consumption of those "poor dishes," which, even statistically, allowed one to remain in good health and live to old age. He coined the term "Mediterranean Diet" for this lifestyle.

A DIET LINKED TO TERRITORY AND LIFESTYLE

The Living Museum of the Mediterranean Diet, based in Pioppi, today celebrates Ancel Keys' many years of work. It is an educational institution made up of exhibition rooms, laboratories, gardens, installations for taste, touch and smell, a room dedicated to home-made pasta, and, last but not least, Ancel Keys' personal library, donated by his family.

The work of the great American scientist proved to be the scientific basis on which UNESCO, in 2010, inscribed the Mediterranean diet into its Representative List of Intangible Cultural Heritage of Humanity. It described the diet as "much more than a simple list of foods [...] it is based on a respect for the territory and biodiversity, and guarantees the conservation and development of traditional activities and crafts linked to fishing and agriculture in Mediterranean communities."

The Chefchaouen Charter, included in the UNESCO document, identifies seven communities in which the Mediterranean diet is still alive, transmitted, protected, and celebrated. These communities, defined as "emblematic," are Pollica in Italy, Koroni in Greece, Soria in Spain, Chefchaouen in Morocco, Agros in Cyprus, Tavira in Portugal, and the islands of Brač and Hvar in Croatia.

A SUSTAINABLE CHOICE

Over the decades, numerous scientific studies, conducted in various countries, have confirmed that the Mediterranean diet benefits people's overall wellbeing, and that pasta accompanied by legumes, vegetables, and fish is a gateway to a tasty, healthy diet that is accessible to all. And not only is it good for people, but it's also good for the planet: according to a World Wildlife Fund (World Wide Fund for Nature) study, a 3½ oz/100 g plate of pasta with tomato sauce has a carbon footprint of just 17 oz/0.492 kg. Cereals, fruits, vegetables, and legumes have a much less intensive need for natural resources than a diet based on meat and animal fats. Healthy eating and environmental sustainability can finally go together.

GLUTEN FREE EGG LASAGNE WITH CLAMS AND MONKFISH

The ancient Romans called them "lagane"—layers of pasta thin enough to make the poets cry. This recipe for an abundant fish sauce is guaranteed to evoke unexpected emotions. Now there's no need to wait for Sunday to enjoy a plate of lasagne.

1 hour   1 hour

SERVES 4

8 sheets gluten free egg lasagne
3 tablespoons plus 1½ teaspoons
    extra virgin olive oil, plus extra
    for drizzling
10½ oz/300 g clams, cleaned
    (see page 57)
1 clove garlic, peeled and whole
⅓ cup (3½ fl oz/100 ml) white wine
1 bunch parsley, finely chopped
1 dried chili pepper, crumbled
4¼ oz/120 g cherry tomatoes,
    cut into wedges
12¼ oz/350 g monkfish fillet,
    finely diced
8 shrimp (prawn) tails, finely
    diced
salt and freshly ground black
    pepper

FOR THE VELOUTÉ
2½ tablespoons (1¼ oz/35 g)
    butter
3 tablespoons cornstarch
    (cornflour)
2 cups (17 fl oz/500 ml) fish broth
    (stock)

Heat the oil in a pan over medium heat, add the clams with the garlic clove, white wine, some of the chopped parsley, and the chili pepper, and cook for 3–4 minutes until the clams open. Remove the clams from their shells and strain the liquid into a bowl.

In a separate pan over high heat, sauté the cherry tomatoes with a drizzle of olive oil for 2–3 minutes, then put them to one side.

Sauté the monkfish and shrimp (prawns) briefly in the same pan for 2 minutes, then add the cherry tomatoes, adjust salt and pepper to taste, add the remaining chopped parsley and the clams, and cook for 2 minutes.

For the velouté, melt the butter in a saucepan, taking care it doesn't change color. Add the cornstarch (cornflour) and whisk until you get a smooth, uniform mixture. Pour in the broth (stock) and the reserved clam liquid and whisk together, taking care to avoid clumps. Bring to the boil and simmer for 1 minute.

Preheat the oven to 350°F (180°C/Gas Mark 4). Spread a layer of the velouté on the bottom of a greased baking dish, cover with a layer of pasta, then another layer of the velouté and the fish sauce. Repeat this procedure until all the ingredients have been used up, ending with a layer of velouté and fish sauce. Cook for around 20 minutes, until bubbling and golden, then leave to cool for 5–10 minutes before serving.

Tip
This recipe can also be prepared with green egg lasagne. Alternatively, the fish sauce can be served with any kind of durum wheat pasta.

GLUTEN FREE PENNE RIGATE WITH TUB GURNARD AND CHERRY TOMATOES

The tub gurnard tells a tale of fishermen and the sea. It is high in mineral salts and low in fat, and together with the cherry tomatoes, oregano, and the sour touch of lemon, creates a simple but tasty sauce.

30 min   15 min

SERVES 4

12¼ oz/350 g gluten free penne rigate or whole grain (wholemeal) caserecce
4 tablespoons extra virgin olive oil
1 clove garlic, finely chopped
7 oz/200 g cherry tomatoes, cut into wedges
1 sprig fresh oregano
17½ oz/500 g tub gurnard or hake fillets, chopped
grated zest of 1 unwaxed lemon
salt and freshly ground black pepper

Heat the oil in a pan over medium heat and add the garlic. Cook for 2 minutes until browned, then add the cherry tomatoes and oregano and cook for 10 minutes.

Add the chopped fish fillets to the tomato sauce with a little salt and pepper, leave to cook for a few minutes, then add the lemon zest.

Cook the pasta in plenty of salted, boiling water according to the packet instructions. Drain when al dente, and toss with the sauce and a grinding of black pepper.

Tip
To lend the final dish a touch of color, blanch 3½ oz/100 g shelled peas for a few minutes in salted, boiling water, then add to the pan of sauce.

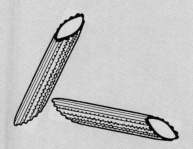

GLUTEN FREE SPAGHETTI WITH SEAFOOD

A typical summer dish to cook as the sun sets over the horizon and the sails return to the harbor. Or perfect served on Christmas Eve, embraced in the warmth of the hearth. Every season is perfect for this traditional Italian classic.

30 min   20 min

SERVES 4

11 oz/320 g gluten free spaghetti
   or legume spaghetti
3 tablespoons plus 1½ teaspoons
   extra virgin olive oil
1 clove garlic, chopped
1 chili pepper, chopped
1 tablespoon chopped parsley
2 tablespoons tomato paste
   (purée), mixed with 1
   tablespoon warm water
3½ oz/100 g baby squid, cleaned
   (see page 60)
3½ oz/100 g small cuttlefish,
   cleaned (see page 60)
3½ oz/100 g langoustine tails
17½ oz/500 g mussels, cleaned
   (see page 70)
17½ oz/500 g clams, cleaned
   (see page 57)
salt

Heat the oil in a skillet (frying pan) over medium heat and, when hot, add the garlic, chili pepper, and parsley. Cook for 2 minutes until the garlic is browned, then add the diluted tomato paste (purée). Cook for 2 minutes, then add the squid and cuttlefish. Cook for 5 minutes, then add the langoustine tails, mussels, and clams. Add a little salt to taste, place a lid over the pan, and continue cooking until the mussels and clams are open, 3–4 minutes.

In the meantime, cook the pasta in plenty of salted, boiling water according to the packet instructions. Then drain when al dente, combine with the sauce, stir and serve.

Tip
Add ⅓ cup (2 oz/50 g) cooked chickpeas to the sauce before serving: they are an excellent accompaniment to a seafood sauce like this one.

WHOLE GRAIN CASARECCE WITH SEABASS RAGÙ

Imagine Kate Winslet and Leonardo DiCaprio, inseparable even off set. Here, the suave seabass and overly confident bell pepper introduce themselves as a couple to the casarecce and agree to dance.

30 min   10 min

SERVES 4

11 oz/320 g whole grain (wholemeal) casarecce or gluten free spaghetti
2¾ tablespoons extra virgin olive oil
7 oz/200 g scallions (spring onions), sliced
1 clove garlic, peeled and whole
25 oz/700 g seabass fillet, diced
9 oz/250 g red bell pepper, diced
⅓ cup (3½ fl oz/100 ml) white wine
salt and freshly ground black pepper

Heat the oil in a pan, add the scallions (spring onions) and whole garlic clove, and leave to cook for 2–3 minutes. Add the diced seabass and bell pepper and leave to cook for another 2 minutes.

Add salt and pepper to taste, then add the white wine and simmer until reduced and the wine has evaporated. Discard the garlic and keep the sauce warm off the heat.

Cook the pasta in plenty of salted, boiling water according to the packet instructions. Drain when al dente, and garnish with the seabass and pepper sauce.

Tip
You can substitute the red bell pepper with the same quantity of zucchini (courgettes), either diced or cut into thin rounds. To add a splash of color, garnish with zucchini (courgette) blossoms that have been sautéed for a few seconds in olive oil.

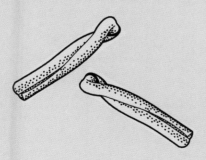

WHOLE GRAIN CASARECCE
WITH SCALLOPS AND PUMPKIN

40 min   20 min

SERVES 4

12¼ oz/350 g whole grain
    (wholemeal) casarecce or
    spaghetti
10½ oz/300 g pumpkin flesh, diced
1 onion, peeled and sliced
1 tablespoon plus 1½ teaspoons
    extra virgin olive oil
1 clove garlic, peeled and whole
1 sprig rosemary, plus a few extra
    leaves to serve
12 scallops, cleaned and diced
Modena balsamic vinegar,
    to serve
salt and freshly ground
    black pepper

Put 3½ oz/100 g of the pumpkin flesh into a pan with the
onion and a pinch of salt. Pour in 3 cups (24 oz/750 ml)
water and bring to a boil. Cook for 15 minutes, then use an
immersion blender to blend until creamy. If necessary, add
a little of the cooking water for medium thickness.

Heat a little oil in a pan over medium heat and add the
garlic clove and the rosemary sprig. Sauté the remaining
pumpkin for 5 minutes, adjusting salt and pepper to taste.
Set aside.

In the same pan, cook the scallops for 1 minute on each
side, then add salt and pepper, the pumpkin cream, and the
sautéed pumpkin cubes.

In the meantime, cook the pasta in plenty of salted, boiling
water according to the packet instructions. Drain when al
dente, and add to the pan. Cook everything together for
a couple of minutes, then serve with a drizzle of balsamic
vinegar and a few rosemary leaves.

TRADITIONAL BALSAMIC VINEGAR

A fine Emilian culinary condiment with great aromatic complexity, Traditional Balsamic Vinegar of Modena PDO (Protected Designation of Origin) has its roots in Roman times. The production process begins with the slow cooking of high-quality grapes such as Trebbiano and Lambrusco Grasparossa. Once cooked, the must is placed in wooden barrels for aging, and undergoes a process of fermentation and progressive dehydration, during which it is decanted along rows of barrels—called batteries—of different sizes and woods. This period of maturation requires a wide temperature range—a very cold environment in winter and a very hot one in summer, and can last from a minimum of twelve years and up to a maximum of thirty years, developing a com-plexity of unique flavors and aromas, and acquiring notes of wood, ripe fruit, and spices.

The vinegar has a dark shade, ranging from mahogany to black, a syrupy consistency, and a viscosity that makes it suitable for adding to dishes as a drizzle. Its sweet and sour flavor embellishes first courses and salads, and it is also an excellent companion to cheeses, fruits (especially strawberries), and even ice cream.

WHOLE GRAIN FARFALLE WITH CHERRY TOMATOES, CAPERS, OLIVES, AND MONKFISH

15 min   10 min

SERVES 4

11 oz/320 g whole grain
    (wholemeal) farfalle or penne
    rigate
2 tablespoons extra virgin olive oil
1 clove garlic, peeled and whole
10½ oz/300 g monkfish fillet, cut
    into pieces
⅓ cup (3½ fl oz/100 ml) white wine
7 oz/200 g cherry tomatoes, cut
    into wedges
1 anchovy fillet, chopped
½ oz/10 g capers
scant ⅓ cup (1¾ oz/50 g) pitted
    Taggiasca olives
finely chopped parsley, to garnish
salt

Cook the pasta in plenty of lightly salted, boiling water according to the packet instructions.

In the meantime, heat the oil in a pan over medium heat with the garlic clove for 2 minutes. Add the fish and brown briefly, about 2 minutes. Add the white wine and cook until the liquid has evaporated, then add the cherry tomatoes, chopped anchovy, and capers and leave to cook for a few minutes, adding a drop of water if necessary to loosen the sauce. Add the olives, and salt to taste, if necessary.

Drain the pasta when al dente, combine with the sauce, and garnish with a dusting of parsley.

SPAGHETTI IS AN ICON

A STORY OF SPAGHETTI

Spaghetti needs no introduction. It is the Italians' most loved pasta shape. And it is probably thanks to those Italians whose exceptional talent made them famous far beyond national borders, that spaghetti was introduced to and eventually conquered the world.

One of the best-loved Italian artists performing in the Metropolitan Opera House in New York in the first decades of the twentieth century was Neapolitan tenor Enrico Caruso; extremely fond of spaghetti, he would eat it in great abundance and with succulent sauces, according to accounts of the time. Caruso took it upon himself to teach his American friends how to cook and garnish it, yet the dish, still new to New Yorkers at the time, posed a problem: how to eat it? Twist it with a fork alone? Use a spoon as a base on which to twist? One evening while dining, Caruso unexpectedly found himself the center of attention, with those present waiting in silence to see how he would deal with his steaming plate of spaghetti and tomato sauce. Annoyed by the embarrassing situation, the tenor dipped his fork into his plate, took a generous portion, and put it in his mouth, staining his face, tie, and even his suit.

To be fair, there is always the risk of a little splash on the tablecloth, face, or clothes, even when eating less zealously than the tenor, so don't be surprised if—even today—waiters serve your spaghetti accompanied by a large cloth napkin. Take the gesture as an invitation to enjoy it—or any long pasta shape—whole-heartedly, whatever the sauce. You may find spaghetti served with tomato-based sauces such as Amatriciana and Assassina, with seafood, with cream-based sauces, or those with just the right amount of butter or extra virgin olive oil—from Carbonara to Cacio e Pepe, Ligurian pesto to garlic, olive oil, and chili pepper. You can only really give up the bib when served a sumptuous Neapolitan-style spaghetti omelette.

NAPLES AND SPAGHETTI

From the late eighteenth century, the pasta-making industry flourished in Naples, particularly around Gragnano and the towns along the Amalfi Coast. As numerous period prints and paintings testify, it could be bought in kiosks on the streets and eaten with your hands, without sauce, or merely with a sprinkling of pepper and grated Parmigiano—hence the Italian expression "*Come il cacio sui maccheroni*," to describe something good that comes at just the right time.

The legendary hunger of the Neapolitans is also embodied in a character from the Commedia dell'Arte: Pulcinella, always hungry for spaghetti. And iconographic art bears witness to the Naples–spaghetti link, as demonstrated by the prestigious watercolor by Pietro Fabris (active in the second half of the eighteenth century) portraying "Spaghetti Eaters in the Bay of Naples."

THE ICONIC FORM

Spaghettini, spaghetti, spaghetti alla chitarra (with a squared shape), spaghettoni, vermicelli, capelli d'angelo, linguine, bucatini, ziti—these are just some of the variations of long pasta that have been created over time by pasta makers. Long pasta is perfect for adhering to classic tomato sauces, and for bringing life to a myriad of gastronomic fantasies. Spaghetti n. 5 is the most iconic form of Barilla pasta: 10 inches (25 centimetres) in length, and a shape that appears on the tables of homes and restaurants all over the world.

Celebrated in hundreds of films, depicted in millions of photographs, and the protagonist of adverts such as that made in 1985 portraying the famous tenor and orchestra conductor Placido Domingo boarding a train and, in the restaurant carriage where his musicians await, opening the case of his double bass and revealing packets and packets of Spaghetti n. 5, presenting it as *"la forma mas deliciosa de la creatividad italiana"* (the most delicious form of Italian creativity). In 1992, it was the turn of Gérard Depardieu,

directed by Ridley Scott, who in order to calm a heated argument between a couple, cooked them spaghetti with tomato sauce served with basil.

There is a grain of truth in the ironic observation of the twentieth-century writer Giuseppe Prezzolini, author of the book *Maccheroni & C.*, that spaghetti has spread Italian genius throughout the world more than the works of Dante Alighieri. An ambassador of the most authentic Italian spirit, this is the pasta that lengthens both days and nights—is there any doubt about what to cook at midnight with your friends?

As fun as a comedy with Jack Lemmon, as vibrant as Mick Jagger's voice, as iconic as a painting by Andy Warhol, as spectacular as Maradona's footwork, as revolutionary as Pep Guardiola's football, as brilliant as Albert Einstein, as irreverent as a Mel Brooks film, as ready for anything as James Bond, as graceful as Mikhail Baryshnikov, as passionate as the looks between Sophia Loren and Marcello Mastroianni—let yourself be inspired by the recipes you are about to read. It's not just spaghetti, but threads of love binding distant stories together.

SPAGHETTONI WITH ASPARAGUS CARBONARA

15 min   13 min

SERVES 4

11 oz/320 g spaghettoni
   or bucatini
5 egg yolks
4¼ oz/120 g Pecorino Romano,
   grated
⅓ cup (3fl oz/80 ml) milk
3 tablespoons extra virgin olive oil
5¼ oz/150 g asparagus, cleaned
   and cut into rounds
2 oz/60 g scallions (spring
   onions), thinly sliced
salt and freshly ground
   black pepper

In a bowl, mix together the egg yolks, a little salt, one-third of the grated Pecorino, and the milk.

Heat the oil in a pan over medium heat and sauté the asparagus together with the scallions (spring onions) for 2–3 minutes until softened.

In the meantime, cook the pasta in plenty of salted, boiling water according to the packet instructions. Drain when al dente, retaining a little of the cooking water, and pour into the pan with the asparagus.

Off the heat, add the egg yolk and Pecorino mixture and 2 tablespoons of the cooking water to the pasta. Stir for 30 seconds. Add the remaining Pecorino, stir well, and serve with freshly ground black pepper.

SPAGHETTONI WITH GARLIC, OIL, AND CHILI PEPPER

15 min   12 min

SERVES 4

11 oz/320 g spaghettoni or
   Spaghetti n. 5
⅓ cup (3½ fl oz/100 ml) extra
   virgin olive oil
4 cloves garlic, peeled and whole
1 fresh red chili pepper, deseeded
   and chopped
finely chopped parsley, to garnish
salt

Heat the oil in a pan over medium heat and, once hot, add the garlic cloves and chopped chili pepper, and fry for 2 minutes.

In the meantime, cook the pasta in plenty of salted, boiling water according to the packet instructions, then drain when al dente, garnish with the flavored oil, and finish with the chopped parsley.

ROASTED SPAGHETTI WITH VEGETABLES ON CREAMED BURRATA

1 hour   30 min

SERVES 4

11 oz/320 g Spaghetti n. 3
    or Spaghetti n. 5
14 oz/400 g mixed vegetables
    (zucchini [courgettes], bell
    peppers, scallions [spring
    onions], beets [beetroot]),
    diced
3½ oz/100 g burrata
2 tablespoons plus 1½ teaspoons
    pine nuts
3 tablespoons extra virgin olive oil
1 teaspoon paprika
1 sprig thyme
1 handful of basil and parsley
    leaves
salt and freshly ground
    black pepper

Blanch each vegetable separately in salted, boiling water for 2 minutes, then cool each one immediately in iced water. Transfer them all to a bowl.

Add a little more salt to the water used for the vegetables and cook the spaghettoni according to the packet instructions, draining the pasta 1 minute earlier than the time indicated. Cool under cold running water for about 1 minute.

Blend the burrata in a blender, adding salt and pepper to taste, and put to one side.

Toast the pine nuts in a dry skillet (frying pan) for 2 minutes.

Lightly grease a separate nonstick skillet (frying pan) with a little of the oil, place over medium-high heat, then add the cooled spaghetti. Stir continually until the spaghetti is toasted and crunchy on the outside. Add the paprika and stir through.

Meanwhile, heat 2 tablespoons of oil in another pan and sauté all the vegetables very quickly, together with a couple of tablespoons of water, and salt and pepper to taste. Add the vegetables to the pasta and blend well.

Heat the remaining oil in a skillet and fry the basil and parsley leaves for 1 minute.

Spread a little of the creamed burrata onto each plate and place the pasta in the center, garnishing it with the vegetables, toasted pine nuts, and fried basil and parsley leaves.

BUCATINI IN VEGETABLE SAUCE

The porous surface of the bucatini is the perfect embrace for a sauce made of so many vegetables: a dish of the most elegant simplicity.

20 min   20 min

SERVES 4

11 oz/320 g bucatini or
    Spaghetti n. 5
3 tablespoons extra virgin olive oil
1 small leek, finely sliced
1 celery stalk, diced
1 small carrot, diced
1 zucchini (courgette), diced
1¾ oz/50 g shelled peas
⅓ cup (3½ fl oz/100 ml)
    vegetable broth (stock)
17¾ oz/500 g canned crushed
    tomatoes
6 basil leaves, ripped
salt and freshly ground
    black pepper

Heat the oil in a large pan over medium heat and, once hot, add the vegetables and leave to cook for 2–3 minutes until starting to brown. Pour in the hot broth (stock) and leave to cook for a further 5 minutes.

Pour the crushed tomatoes into the pan, increase the heat to high, and leave to cook for around 10 minutes, adjusting salt and pepper to taste and stirring occasionally.

In the meantime, cook the pasta in plenty of salted, boiling water according to the packet instructions. Drain the pasta when al dente, transfer to a serving dish, and top with the sauce and ripped basil leaves, and serve.

Tips
As an extra topping, add 1 tablespoon pine nuts that have been lightly toasted for 2 minutes in a dry skillet (frying pan).

If you can't get hold of fresh peas, you can use either tinned peas (drain them thoroughly) or frozen peas (blanch them briefly in plenty of salted, boiling water).

BUCATINI WITH SHALLOTS, CHERRY TOMATOES, AND NUTS

A stunning and delicate dish that brings everyone together.
After eating, don't hesitate to grab a piece of fresh bread
to finish off the sauce and clean your plate.

20 min   20 min

SERVES 4

11 oz/320 g bucatini or
    spaghettoni
4 tablespoons extra virgin olive oil
3¾ oz/110 g shallot, sliced
2 lb/900 g cherry tomatoes,
    halved
2 tablespoons pistachios,
    toasted and coarsely chopped
2 tablespoons pine nuts,
    toasted and coarsely chopped
2 tablespoons hazelnuts,
    toasted and coarsely chopped
2 tablespoons julienned basil
salt and freshly ground
    black pepper

Heat the oil in a pan over a medium heat and sauté the
shallot for around 5 minutes, until slightly caramelized.

Increase the heat to high, add the cherry tomatoes, and
leave to cook until collapsing, about 3 minutes, adjusting
salt and pepper to taste.

Cook the pasta in plenty of salted, boiling water according
to the packet instructions. Then drain when al dente, add
to the sauce, and mix together. Top with the nuts and basil,
and serve.

Tip
Use cherry tomatoes of the same size but different colors:
appearance matters!

TOMATO

The tomato plant arrived in Europe from Mexico and Central America in the 1500s. Its fruits, a golden yellow in color, were called *"mela aurea"* or *"pomo d'oro"* (golden apples) by the Italians, and mainly used for ornamental purposes. It would take a couple of centuries for the tomato to be used as a food, as initially it was believed to be poisonous.

There are thousands of varieties of tomato throughout the world, grown wherever the plant can enjoy long periods of heat and sunlight. The flavor varies depending on the degree of acidity, sugar and water content, and pulp texture. In Italy, around 300 varieties are produced and sold, the most common being the San Marzano, oxheart, salad tomato, Pachino, cherry tomato, Datterino, the camone, and the Vesuvius tomato.

There are infinite ways of consuming tomatoes, in both raw and cooked form. An ideal companion for pasta, an indispensable ally on pizza, they go well with beef and veal, and fish such as tuna, sardines, and mullet. They are enhanced by garlic, shallots, basil, thyme, and oregano, and make an excellent appetizer both dried and in oil.

BUCATINI ALLA MONFERRINA

15 min   8 min

SERVES 4

11 oz/320 g bucatini or
    Spaghetti n. 5
scant ½ cup (3½ oz/100 g) butter
½ clove garlic
2 sprigs sage
1 sprig rosemary
1 sprig thyme
1 bay leaf
grated Parmigiano Reggiano, to
    serve
salt

Melt the butter in a pan over low heat with the garlic and herbs, and cook for 2 minutes to allow the ingredients to flavor the butter.

Cook the pasta in plenty of salted, boiling water according to the packet instructions. Drain when al dente and mix with the flavored butter (discard the garlic and herbs). Serve with a sprinkle of grated Parmigiano.

Tip
To enrich this sauce, you can add asparagus tips blanched for a few minutes in salted boiling water, or you can add crunch with a spoonful of lightly toasted hazelnuts.

BAVETTE WITH BAGNA CAUDA
AND CRUNCHY VEGETABLES

20 min   20 min

SERVES 4

11 oz/320 g bavette or
 Spaghetti n. 5
4 cloves garlic, peeled and whole
scant 1 cup (7 fl oz/200 ml) whole
 (full-fat) milk
6 tablespoons extra virgin olive oil
5 anchovy fillets
1–1½ oz/30–40 g beurre manié (see
 Tip)
4 small zucchini (courgettes),
 cut into rounds
4 asparagus spears, cleaned and
 cut on the diagonal
8 oz/225 g celery hearts,
 cut on the diagonal
1 tablespoon finely chopped
 parsley
salt

Place the garlic cloves in a pan with the milk over low heat. Bring to a simmer, cook for 10 minutes, then drain, reserving the garlic.

Heat the oil in a small saucepan over low heat and fry the garlic and the anchovies for 2 minutes, then blend together and pass through a sieve to get a velouté.

In a saucepan, bring the velouté to a boil, then remove from the heat once melted, thickening the bagna cauda with a little beurre manié if necessary.

In the meantime, cook the pasta according to the packet instructions, adding the vegetables a few minutes before the end of the cooking time, then drain when al dente and mix with the bagna cauda. Garnish the dish with the parsley.

Tip
For homemade beurre manié, mix equal parts butter and flour until you have a creamy consistency. It is ideal for thickening sauces and gravies.

SPAGHETTI RIGATI WITH WALNUT SAUCE

25 min   10 min

SERVES 4

11 oz/320 g spaghetti rigati
   or Spaghetti n. 5
½ cup (1¾ oz/50 g) shelled walnuts
1 piece of day-old white bread
   (around 1 oz/25 g)
⅓ cup (3½ fl oz/100 ml) milk, plus
   extra if needed
½ oz/15 g pine nuts
⅓ cup (3½ fl oz/100 ml) extra
   virgin olive oil
¾ oz/20 g Parmigiano Reggiano,
   grated
1 clove garlic, peeled and whole
1 teaspoon marjoram leaves,
   to garnish
salt

Blanch the walnuts in boiling water for 2–3 minutes, then remove their skins.

Discard the crust from the bread, then dip and soak the bread in the milk. Squeeze out any excess liquid, then transfer the bread to a blender with the remaining ingredients (except the marjoram), and blend until you get a smooth-textured sauce; if necessary, add another drop of milk.

Cook the pasta in plenty of salted, boiling water according to the packet instructions. Drain when al dente, retaining a little of the pasta cooking water, then transfer to a serving dish and top with the walnut sauce, diluting it, if necessary, with a little of the cooking water. Garnish with the marjoram leaves, and serve.

SPAGHETTI: THE ORIGIN OF THE SHAPE

THE HISTORY OF SPAGHETTI

What are the origins of this pasta that is so loved all over the world? They have been lost in the mists of time—and perhaps that isn't so important, because, at the end of the day, spaghetti is a "technical" shape, long and cylindrical, the result of pulling, invented and reinvented in different times and places.

What is certain is that in Italy from the Renaissance period, pasta was produced with a machine—the torque—and a die, and spaghetti was most likely the first shape to come from the new device.

In Naples, the most important company dedicated to the production of pasta was born: the Guild of Neapolitan Vermicellari, which broke away from the bakers guild and took its name from vermicelli, the oldest record of which dates back to 1571. It was again in Naples that, in the 1700s, spaghetti was crowned as the most popular and loved shape.

As always, behind the success of any dish there is a convergence of very concrete interests. First of all the people, who had to feed themselves on limited means. Then the producers, during a period when large landowners in the kingdoms of Naples and Sicily sold grain relatively cheaply, making pasta a food accessible to many. Pasta also proved to be optimal for bypassing religious requirements, when the consumption of meat was prohibited, with the obligation to eat lean foods. Then there were industrial interests, which in Naples went hand in hand with technological progress and the advent of more evolved and larger machinery, which could offer a better yield.

THE EVOLUTION OF SPAGHETTI

You may be wondering when spaghetti got its name.

It was 1879 when the *Dictionary of the Italian Language* by Niccolò Tommaseo and Bernardo Bellini, in the listing for "Spaghetto, singular masculine diminutive of SPAGO," included the line "Spaghetti Minestra: pasta the size of small string and long, like sopraccapellini."

And its union with tomato? In 1839, Ippolito Cavalcanti, Duke of Bonvicino, in his *Cucina Teorico Pratica*, first codifies in the Neapolitan dialect "i vermicielli co' le pommodore," the first recipe for spaghetti with tomato sauce, destined to become the most popular and perhaps the most famous pasta dish in the world. This should have come as no surprise: the tomato, which arrived in Europe in the sixteenth century following the conquest of the Americas, was looked at with distrust for at least a century before it was cultivated in the allotments of Italian farmers.

Before teaming up with the tomato, our beloved spaghetti knew only oil, Parmesan, and pepper. The very first "red" spaghetti can be found in an eighteenth-century Neapolitan nativity scene in the magnificent Royal Palace of Caserta. It was a recipe that would determine the fruits of the plant from the *solanaceae* family as the perfect supreme sauce. An iconic, predestined dish, loved by all, from beggars on the streets of Naples to nobility.

Later on, spaghetti was brought to the American continent in the suitcases of Italian migrants in the hope of softening the pain of being separated from the motherland, contributing to its spread and success across the ocean and eventually throughout the world.

SPAGHETTI CACIO E PEPE SCENTED WITH LEMON

30 min   8 min

SERVES 4

11 oz/320 g Spaghetti n. 5 or
   whole grain (wholemeal)
   spaghetti
1¼ cups/300 ml whole milk
1 teaspoon cornstarch (cornflour)
2¾ oz/80 g Grana Padano,
   medium aged, grated
1¾ oz/50 g Pecorino Romano,
   grated
¾ oz/20 g grated fresh horseradish
grated zest of 1 unwaxed lemon
lemon thyme leaves, to garnish
salt and freshly ground black
   pepper

Cook the pasta in plenty of salted, boiling water according to the packet instructions. Drain when al dente, and leave to cool on a tray.

For the sauce, bring the milk to a boil in a small pan. Stir a little cold water into the cornstarch (cornflour), then stir into the milk together with the Grana Padano and a pinch of salt. Mix well.

Stir the pasta through the sauce and top with the grated Pecorino, horseradish, lemon zest, a few lemon thyme leaves, and black pepper.

SPAGHETTI WITH TOMATO AND BASIL

20 min   10 min

SERVES 4

11 oz/320 g Spaghetti n. 5 or
  whole grain (wholemeal)
  spaghetti
4 tablespoons extra virgin olive oil
1 clove garlic, lightly crushed but
  still whole
2 oz/50 g onion, finely chopped
1 cup (8½ fl oz/250 ml) San
  Marzano tomato purée
  (passata)
1 oz/30 g basil leaves, plus extra
  to garnish
2 oz/50 g Parmigiano Reggiano,
  grated
salt and freshly ground black
  pepper

Cook the pasta in plenty of salted, boiling water according to the packet instructions.

In the meantime, heat 2 tablespoons of oil in a pan, and sauté the garlic and onion for 5 minutes. Add the tomato purée (passata), basil, salt and pepper to taste, and just under a cup (7 fl oz/200 ml) of cooking water from the pasta, and simmer for 5 minutes. Remove and discard the garlic clove.

Drain the pasta when al dente and combine with the tomato sauce. Drizzle over the rest of the oil, and sprinkle with the basil leaves and Parmigiano before serving.

BASIL

This strong-scented aromatic plant was originally from India. The ancient Greeks considered it to be so precious that it was reserved for kings, lending it its name *"basilicos,"* which in Greek means "royal." Used plentifully in Mediterranean cuisine, as well as in many Asian ones, its flavor changes depending on the variety, assuming nuances of lemon, jasmine, cloves, aniseed, or thyme. It is picked before blossoming to retain its flavor, and emits a fresh, intense fragrance, with aromatic notes from the sweet to the slightly bitter.

There are around sixty varieties of basil throughout the world. In the southern regions of Italy, it is characterized by wide, thick, meaty leaves with a strong, spicy flavor. Genovese Basil PDO (Protected Designation of Origin), the variety that is used for the pesto of the same name, is cultivated along the Tyrrhenian side of the Ligurian coast, which has a particular microclimate and terrain that has given the basil a unique profile; it has small, thin, delicate leaves and a very intense fragrance.

In Italian cuisine, basil is often used alongside tomato, creating an iconic union of flavor, and can be served on or in pasta dishes, salads, eggs, cheeses, vegetables, fish, and seafood.

WHOLE GRAIN SPAGHETTI WITH CREAM OF ASPARAGUS AND GOAT'S CHEESE

With its full, sweet, persistent flavor, goat's cheese is the perfect balance to the bitter taste of asparagus. The whole grain (wholemeal) spaghetti presents the dish to the public, awaiting admiration and approval.

30 min   20 min

SERVES 4

11 oz/320 g whole grain
    (wholemeal) spaghetti or
    spaghettoni
10 oz/300 g asparagus, cleaned
    and cut into rounds, tips
    reserved
2 tablespoons extra virgin olive oil
1 shallot, chopped
½ clove garlic
a few mint leaves, coarsely
    chopped
a few basil leaves, coarsely
    chopped
2¾ oz/80 g fresh goat's cheese
salt and freshly ground black
    pepper

Blanch the asparagus tips in salted, boiling water for 2 minutes, then plunge into a bowl of iced water. Keep ½ cup (4 fl oz/120 ml) of the cooking water to one side.

Heat the oil in a pan over medium heat and cook the shallot and garlic clove for 3–4 minutes, until browned. Add the asparagus rounds, adjusting salt and pepper to taste, and then add the chopped mint and basil leaves. Pour the cooking water from the asparagus tips into the pan and leave to cook for 10 minutes, then leave to cool slightly. Blend to a sauce consistency using an immersion blender.

Cook the pasta in plenty of salted, boiling water according to the packet instructions. Drain when al dente, and transfer to the pan with the cream of asparagus and the asparagus tips and cook for a couple of minutes. Serve with a spoonful of fresh goat's cheese per person.

Tip
For a more consistent cream, add 3 tablespoons toasted blanched almonds to the blender. For an even fresher dish, grate over a little lemon zest before serving.

SPAGHETTONI WITH LOCUST LOBSTER, CHERRY TOMATOES, AND BOTTARGA

Small European locust lobsters are the perfect ingredient for a delicate broth for spaghettoni. The bottarga brings with it the intense flavor of the sea. Close your eyes, breathe in, and take a bite.

70 min   1 hour

SERVES 4

11 oz/320 g spaghettoni or
    Spaghetti n. 5
30 cherry tomatoes, halved
brown sugar, for sprinkling
extra virgin olive oil, for drizzling
4 small European locust lobsters,
    cleaned and shelled (shells
    reserved for the broth)
1¾ oz/50 g mullet bottarga, finely
    grated
1 oz/25 g butter
garlic oil, for drizzling
chili oil, for drizzling
finely chopped parsley, to garnish
salt

FOR THE BROTH
3 tablespoons extra virgin olive oil
1 carrot, finely chopped
1 celery stalk, finely chopped
1 onion, finely chopped
aromatics (bay leaves, juniper
    berries, peppercorns, fennel
    seeds), for seasoning

Preheat the oven to 210°F (100°C/Gas Mark ½).

Place the tomatoes on a sheet pan (baking tray), cut-side up. Sprinkle with a little salt, the brown sugar, and a drizzle of extra virgin olive oil, then cook for 1 hour.

For the broth (stock), heat the oil in a pan over medium heat and add the lobster shells, leaving them to cook for 5 minutes.

Add the finely chopped carrot, celery, and onion and cook for a further 3 minutes. Add the aromatics, and cover with 4 pints (2 liters) of cold water. Bring everything to a simmer—to 190°F (90°C), if you have a thermometer—and cook for 20 minutes. Strain the broth and put to one side.

In a large nonstick pan, bring to the boil 4 cups (34 fl oz/ 1 liter) of broth, ¼ oz/10g grated bottarga, and 1 teaspoon of salt. Add the spaghettoni and stir gently. Cook for around 7 minutes, adding more broth if necessary. Add the lobster flesh and cooked tomatoes. Add the butter and a drizzle of garlic and chili oils. Garnish the dish with the remaining bottarga and finely chopped parsley.

Tip
You can also garnish this dish with parsley oil: blanch 1 oz/30 g parsley in salted, boiling water for a few seconds and leave to cool. Blend the parsley for 6 minutes with extra virgin olive oil (enough to cover the parsley). Strain through a fine-meshed sieve into a bowl placed over ice to keep the bright green color. You can also freeze the parsley oil and use for other recipes.

SPAGHETTI WITH SEABASS, GREEN PESTO, AND POTATOES

25 min   15 min

SERVES 4

11 oz/320 g Spaghetti n. 5
    or bucatini
2 tablespoons extra virgin olive oil
1 potato, peeled and diced
10 cherry tomatoes, cut into
    wedges
7 oz/200 g seabass fillets
¾ cup (7 oz/200 g) basil pesto
1 sprig basil, leaves picked
salt

Heat the oil in a pan and sauté the potatoes for 10 minutes, leaving them crunchy. Put to one side.

In the same pan, fry the cherry tomato wedges and the seabass fillets for around 5 minutes, breaking up the fillets with a wooden spoon. Put to one side.

In the meantime, cook the pasta in plenty of lightly salted, boiling water according to the packet instructions. Drain when al dente, then tip into the pan with the sauce. Mix well, remove from the heat, and stir through the pesto.

Finally, add the crunchy potato cubes and basil leaves before serving.

GLUTEN FREE SPAGHETTI SALAD
WITH RED SHRIMP AND BURRATA

1 hour   8 min

SERVES 4

11 oz/320 g gluten free spaghetti
   or whole grain (wholemeal)
   spaghetti
8 red shrimp (prawn) tails
grated zest of 1 unwaxed lemon
½ oz/10 g wild fennel, plus extra
   sprigs to garnish
2 cups (17 fl oz/500 ml)
   dry white wine
1½ oz/40 g coarse salt
7 oz/200 g fennel bulb
2¾ tablespoons extra virgin
   olive oil
4 oz/120 g burrata
freshly ground black pepper

Clean the shrimp (prawns), putting the shell, heads, and tails to one side. Squeeze the heads to remove the juices and put the juices to one side.

Bring to the boil 3 pints (1.5 liters) of water with half the grated lemon zest, the shells and heads of the shrimp, and the wild fennel, then add the white wine and half the coarse salt, then cook the spaghetti according to packet instructions until al dente.

Drain and cool the pasta in salted cold water (use the remaining coarse salt) briefly so it doesn't lose the aroma and depth of flavor.

In the meantime, juice the fennel until you have about 3 tablespoons of juice. Using an immersion blender, blend the juice with the oil and the juice obtained from the shrimp heads until you have a thick sauce.

Cut the shrimp tails into cubes (around ¼ inch/4 mm) and leave to marinate in the blended juices for a few moments.

Cut the burrata in half to obtain the stracciatella inside.

Dry the spaghetti in a dish (tea) towel and combine with the sauce, the shrimp tartare, and a few sprigs of wild fennel.

Create nest shapes with the garnished pasta, placing them in the pasta bowls. Complete each with 1 oz/30 g burrata stracciatella, a little grated lemon zest, and some ground black pepper.

MOVIES, ART, AND... SPAGHETTI

Movies and spaghetti—what a great couple. And where did this tasty artistic union begin? In Rome, in 1927. Indeed, the first meeting between pasta and the movie world took place outside of the set and was an extraordinary success. The protagonists were the famous Hollywood couple and stars of silent movies, Mary Pickford and Douglas Fairbanks, and the Roman chef, Alfredo di Lelio, inventor of the Fettuccine Alfredo, destined to become so popular throughout the world.

The three had already met in 1920 when the two actors, on their honeymoon in Rome, had enjoyed the fettuccine dish with butter and Parmigiano that the chef had invented at home to revive his convalescent wife. Seven years later, the two actors are once more at Alfredo's on Via della Scrofa, in the center of Rome, but this time they bring as a gift some gold cutlery with a dedication: "To Alfredo, the King of noodles." News of the visit and the gift soon traveled around the globe, and for Alfredo no advertising could have been more effective. The dish was set to become incredibly popular all over the world.

ONSCREEN APPEARANCES

"Life is a combination of pasta and magic," said the great Federico Fellini, and many critics agree that the most iconic scene of 1960's *La Dolce Vita* is not "Marcello, come here," but rather the one in which Anita Ekberg says, "Spaghetti carbonara: one, two, three!". In fact, the liaison between spaghetti carbonara and the dolce vita was already in full swing in the 1950s, and, perhaps because of the American version with bacon, it managed to find its way into the hearts, and stomachs, of film stars, from Gregory Peck to Oliver Hardy, and from Mamie Van Doren to Sophia Loren, thus establishing a strong culinary axis between Italy and the United States, where dozens of recipes for the famous dish were published.

In its simplicity, spaghetti soon became one of the most recognizable and magnetic symbols of a generous, delicious, light-hearted, and perhaps even provocative Italian spirit—think "Maccarone, did you provoke me?" in Alberto Sordi's famous scene in *An American in Rome*—to the point that Italian cinema would use it abundantly. In low-budget Italian films the director often introduces a plate of spaghetti to a scene to bring joy and symbolically chase away the memories of the hunger suffered during wartime. One of the most important is the scene from *Poverty and Nobility* (1954), in which the actor Totò stands on the table and grabs spaghetti, gulping down as much as he can and stuffing it into his overcoat pockets.

Even Hollywood screenwriters realized that spaghetti could combine both taste and passion. In 1955's *Lady and the Tramp*, a thin thread of pasta unites two distant worlds—that of the bourgeois dog Lady and the stray Tramp—and ends in a kiss that would make cinematic history. We also find Jack Lemmon and Shirley MacLaine struggling with spaghetti in Billy Wilder's *The Apartment* (1960). One of the funniest scenes in the film is the one in which Lemmon finds nothing better than a tennis racket to drain the spaghetti with meatballs, a classic of Italian-American cuisine, and a dish featured in many more American films, including Martin Scorsese's masterpiece, *Goodfellas* (1990).

Spaghetti even lent its name to a cinematic genre—spaghetti westerns—films shot with small budgets and semi-unknown, yet strongly characterized, actors. Initially snubbed by critics, spaghetti westerns gradually conquered a growing audience worldwide, reaching epic heights, thanks to the genius of Sergio Leone and Ennio Morricone and legendary performers such as Clint Eastwood, Lee Van Cleef, and Eli Wallach.

SPAGHETTI IN ART

Could spaghetti perhaps escape the careful eye of artists? Certainly not. The first artist to paint it was the Dutchman Mathias Stomer in the seventeenth century, in the painting "Il Mangiamaccheroni," now in the Capodimonte Museum in Naples. A Naples that, in the eighteenth and nineteenth centuries, saw a flourishing of minor designers and artists who depicted scenes of daily life dealing with spaghetti. In 1956, the expressionist painter Renato Guttuso painted "The Man Who Eats Spaghetti," inspired by his father. The work depicts a Sicilian fisherman returning from the sea who greedily eats a plate of spaghetti and, with his left hand, seems to want to keep the bowl close and protect it from the attentions of others. In the United States, James Rosenquist with "I Love You with my Ford" (1961) and Yayoi Kusama with "Handbag Macaroni" (1965) represent the famous format accompanied with lots of red tomatoes. In 1958, Andy Warhol created "Spaghetti Is So Slippery," and in 1986 he created "Campbell's Soup Box—Chicken Noodle." Nothing is more iconic than spaghetti—even in contemporary art.

BUCATINI WITH CRAB

30 min   10 min

SERVES 4

11 oz/320 g bucatini or
   Spaghetti n. 5
3 tablespoons extra virgin olive oil
1 clove garlic, peeled and whole
8¾ oz/250 g white crabmeat
generous ¾ cup (7 fl oz/200 ml)
   brandy
5½ oz/150 g cherry tomatoes,
   cut into wedges
1 fresh or dried red chili pepper
4 tablespoons heavy (double)
   cream
1 tablespoon finely chopped
   parsley
salt and freshly ground black
   pepper

Heat the oil with the garlic clove in a large pan for
2 minutes until the oil is flavored. Add the crabmeat
and brandy, then leave to simmer until the brandy has
evaporated, 3–4 minutes.

Add the tomatoes, cook until shriveled a little, then add
the chili pepper and cream. Discard the garlic clove, bring
to a boil, then leave to one side.

In the meantime, cook the pasta in plenty of salted, boiling
water according to the packet instructions. Drain when al
dente, reserving a little of the cooking water, then tip the
pasta into the pan of sauce.

Stir well, adding the parsley, a grinding of black pepper,
and, if necessary, a little of the cooking water to loosen.

LINGUINE WITH CHERRY TOMATOES AND SEAFOOD

1 hour   20 min

SERVES 4

11 oz/320 g linguine
   or spaghettoni
3 tablespoons extra virgin olive oil
1 clove garlic, finely chopped
2 tablespoons chopped parsley,
   plus extra to garnish
1 bunch basil, leaves ripped
1 sprig oregano, leaves picked
14 oz/400 g mussels, cleaned
   (see page 70)
14 oz/400 g clams, cleaned
   (see page 57)
⅔ cup (5 fl oz/150 ml) white wine
4 red mullet, gutted, filleted,
   and deboned
4 langoustines
4 shrimp (prawns), shelled
5¼ oz/150 g cherry tomatoes,
   quartered
salt and freshly ground black
   pepper

Heat the oil in a pan over medium heat with the garlic, parsley, basil, and oregano leaves for 2 minutes. Add the mussels, clams, and the white wine. Cover and wait for the mussels and clams to open, 3–4 minutes. Once open, remove and discard the shells from around three-quarters of them, and put all the mussels and clams in a bowl.

In the same pan, cook the red mullet, the whole langoustines, the shelled shrimp (prawns), and cherry tomatoes. Leave to cook for a few minutes, then add the mussels and clams to the sauce. Adjust salt and pepper to taste. The sauce should still be quite liquid at the end of cooking.

Cook the pasta in plenty of salted, boiling water according to the packet instructions. Drain when al dente, then add to the pan with the fish sauce and cook for a couple of minutes. Garnish with chopped parsley.

CLAMS

Clams are bivalve mollusks that live on the sandy bottom of the brackish waters of the Mediterranean Sea and eastern Atlantic. They have a variegated color ranging from gray to brown, with concentric dark streaks. Their characteristic elliptical shape gives them an elegant and distinctive appearance.

Their prized gastronomic quality makes clams one of the undisputed protagonists of Italian cuisine. From a culinary point of view, they are a delicacy due to their light and tasty meat, which is used in the preparation of many seafood dishes, including the famous Spaghetti alle Vongole. Versatile, tender, and with a distinctive flavor, over the years they have acquired a prominent place in Mediterranean culinary culture.

They are collected following precise regulations to guarantee their sustainability—a careful management of marine resources, which has proved decisive in preserving the population of these mollusks and guaranteeing their presence on fine-dining menus around the world.

SPAGHETTONI SCENTED WITH MUSKY OCTOPUS

A masterpiece of simplicity and taste with which to enchant your guests, thanks to the fragrance of the seafood and the intense flavor of the tomatoes, peppers, and basil.

70 min   1 hour

SERVES 4

11 oz/320 g spaghettoni
  or bucatini
7 oz/200 g vine tomatoes,
  cut in half and deseeded
3 cloves garlic, peeled and whole
⅓ oz/10 g thyme
scant 1 tablespoon brown sugar
3 tablespoons extra virgin olive oil,
  plus extra for drizzling
2¼ lb/1 kg musky octopus, cleaned
  and ink sacs set aside
1 cup (8½ fl oz/250 ml) white wine
1 red bell pepper
2 fresh red chili peppers
3½ oz/100 g basil leaves
1 scallion (spring onion)
salt

Preheat the oven to 250°F (120°C/Gas Mark ½).

For the confit tomatoes: place the tomatoes in a baking dish and toss with 1 clove garlic, half the thyme, the brown sugar, salt to taste, and a drizzle of oil. Cook in the oven for 1 hour.

In the meantime, lay the octopus in a large pan, add the wine and another garlic clove, cover, and cook on low heat for 25–30 minutes. Strain the cooking liquid into a pan and add 2 fl oz/50 ml ink from the octopus sacs. Put the liquid and octopus to one side.

Preheat the oven to 285°F (140°C/Gas Mark 1). For the red sauce: brush the red pepper and chili peppers with 2 tablespoons of oil, cover with foil, and cook for 1 hour. Cut all the peppers in half on a chopping board and remove the seeds. Peel gently, cut them into pieces, then cook in a pot, covered, over low heat for 10–15 minutes. Blend to a sauce in a blender. Set aside.

For the green sauce: blanch the basil leaves in salted, boiling water for a few seconds, then cool in iced water. Squeeze the moisture out of the leaves, then garnish with a drizzle of oil. Blend in a blender and set aside.

In a griddle pan, cook the octopus with 1 tablespoon of oil, the garlic and thyme, pressing down with a palette knife to make it crunchier.

Cook the pasta in plenty of salted, boiling water for 4–5 minutes, then drain and finish cooking in the black octopus liquid for another 4–5 minutes. Remove the pan from the heat and mix well until you get a creamy texture, adding a drizzle of oil. Add the confit tomatoes, sliced thinly. Serve the pasta with the two sauces and the musky octopus.

BUCATINI ALLA CACCIATORA

Bucatini elevates the thick, flavorsome rabbit sauce. A dish to fall in love with, and one that must be enjoyed at least once in a lifetime.

30 min   20 min

SERVES 4

11 oz/320 g bucatini or whole grain (wholemeal) spaghetti
2 tablespoons extra virgin olive oil
2 oz/60 g pancetta, chopped
2½ oz/75 g onion, sliced
1 clove garlic, peeled and whole
1 sprig sage, leaves picked
1 sprig rosemary, leaves picked
½ rabbit, deboned and flesh cut into pieces
3 tablespoons plus 1½ teaspoons Marsala
14 oz/400 g canned peeled tomatoes, puréed
1½ oz/40 g Parmigiano Reggiano, grated
salt and freshly ground black pepper

Heat the oil in a pan on medium heat, add the chopped pancetta, the onion, the garlic clove, and the sage and rosemary leaves, and cook for 5 minutes until browned.

Add the rabbit pieces and leave to brown for a few minutes, then pour in the Marsala. Let the liquid evaporate, then pour in the puréed peeled tomatoes. Adjust salt and pepper to taste and leave to cook over a low flame for about 20 minutes. If the sauce becomes too dry, add a few ladlefuls of hot water. Remove the garlic clove at the end of cooking.

Cook the pasta in plenty of salted, boiling water according to the packet instructions. Drain when al dente, toss with the rabbit sauce, and serve with a generous helping of grated Parmigiano.

BUCATINI WITH DUCK RAGÙ

80 min   30 min

SERVES 4

11 oz/320 g bucatini or
    spaghettoni
⅓ cup (3½ fl oz/100 ml)
    extra virgin olive oil
1 clove garlic, peeled and whole
5¼ oz/150 g soffritto mix (finely
    diced onion, carrot, and celery
    stalk)
1¾ oz/50 g Prosciutto di Parma,
    cut into strips
4 sage leaves, plus extra to
    garnish
1 sprig rosemary, plus extra to
    garnish
8¾ oz/250 g duck breast,
    chopped
⅔ cup (5 fl oz/150 ml)
    red wine
10½ oz/300 g canned crushed
    tomatoes
vegetable or meat broth (stock),
    as needed
salt and freshly ground
    black pepper

Heat half the oil in a pan and fry the garlic clove with the
soffritto mix for 2–3 minutes. Add the Prosciutto, sage,
and rosemary, and continue to cook for 2 minutes.

In a separate pan, heat the remaining oil and brown the
duck for 5 minutes. Add the duck to the vegetable mix with
the red wine and cook until the liquid has evaporated. Add
the crushed tomatoes, salt, and pepper to taste, and cook
for around 30 minutes, adding broth (stock) if necessary.

Cook the pasta in plenty of salted, boiling water according
to the packet instructions. Drain when al dente, toss with
the duck ragù, and garnish with sage and rosemary.

SPAGHETTI WITH ARUGULA AND PROSCIUTTO

30 min   10 min

SERVES 4

11 oz/320 g Spaghetti n. 5
   or spaghettoni
4¾ tablespoons extra virgin
   olive oil
1 shallot, finely chopped
7 oz/200 g Prosciutto di Parma,
   cut into strips
2 lb/900 g cherry tomatoes,
   halved
3½ oz/100 g arugula (rocket)
salt and freshly ground black
   pepper

Heat the oil in a pan over medium heat, add the shallot, and cook for 3 minutes. Increase the heat to high, add the Prosciutto and the cherry tomatoes, and cook for 3 minutes.

In the meantime, cook the pasta in plenty of salted, boiling water according to the packet instructions.

Drain the pasta when al dente, reserving some of the cooking water, and add to the sauce in the pan with a little of the cooking water if necessary to blend well, and the arugula (rocket). Garnish with freshly ground black pepper before serving.

SPAGHETTONI WITH TURKEY, PORCINI MUSHROOMS, AND TRUFFLE

30 min   10 min

SERVES 4

11 oz/320 g spaghettoni or
    bucatini
2 tablespoons extra virgin olive oil
12¼ oz/350 g turkey breast,
    chopped
3½ oz/50 ml heavy (double) cream
finely chopped parsley, plus extra
    to garnish
7 oz/200 g porcini mushrooms,
    cleaned and diced
1 oz/30 g black summer truffle
salt and freshly ground black
    pepper

Heat 1 tablespoon of oil in a pan over medium heat and brown the turkey breast for 5 minutes. Add the cream and finely chopped parsley, and adjust salt and pepper to taste, leaving to cook for 3–4 minutes.

Heat the remaining oil over high heat, and sauté the porcini mushrooms for 3 minutes, stirring continuously.

Cook the pasta in plenty of salted, boiling water according to the packet instructions. Drain when al dente, transfer to a serving dish, top with the turkey sauce and porcini mushrooms, and garnish with slivers of black truffle and a little more parsley, if you wish.

INDEX

RECIPE NOTES

INDEX

D

RECIPE NOTES

Butter should always be unsalted, unless otherwise specified.

All herbs are fresh, unless otherwise specified.

Eggs are medium (US large) unless otherwise specified.

Individual vegetables and fruits, such as onions and apples, are assumed to be medium, unless otherwise specified.

All milk is whole (3% fat), homogenized, and lightly pasteurized, unless otherwise specified.

All salt is fine sea salt, unless otherwise specified.

Exercise a high level of caution when following recipes involving any potentially hazardous activity, including the use of high temperatures, open flames and when deep-frying. In particular, when deep-frying add food carefully to avoid splashing, wear long sleeves and never leave the pan unattended.

Cooking times are for guidance only. If using a fan (convection) oven, follow the manufacturer's instructions concerning the oven temperatures.

All herbs, shoots, flowers and leaves should be picked fresh from a clean source. Do exercise caution when foraging for ingredients, which should only be eaten if an expert has deemed them safe to eat. In particular, do not gather wild mushrooms yourself before seeking the advice of an expert who has confirmed their suitability for human consumption. As some species of mushrooms have been known to cause allergic reaction and illness, do take extra care when cooking and eating mushrooms and do seek immediate medical help if you experience a reaction after preparing or eating them.

Exercise caution when making fermented products, ensuring all equipment is spotlessly clean, and seek expert advice if in any doubt.

When using raw fish in a recipe, consult with your fishmonger to ensure it has been blast-chilled and is fit for consumption raw.

When no quantity is specified, for example of oils, salts and herbs used for finishing dishes, quantities are discretionary and flexible

All spoon and cup measurements are level, unless otherwise stated. 1 teaspoon = 5 ml; 1 tablespoon = 15 ml. Australian standard tablespoons are 20 ml, so Australian readers are advised to use 3 teaspoons in place of 1 tablespoon when measuring small quantities.

Cup, metric, and imperial measurements are used in this book. Follow one set of measurements throughout, not a mixture, as they are not interchangeable.

Phaidon Press Limited
2 Cooperage Yard
London E15 2QR

Phaidon Press Inc.
111 Broadway
New York, NY 10006

phaidon.com

First published 2024
©2024 Phaidon Press Limited

ISBN 978 1 83866 884 6

Commissioning Editor:
  Emilia Terragni
Project Editor: Rachel Malig
Designer: Melanie Mues,
  Mues Design, London
Production Controller:
  Lily Rodgers

Recipe text: Academia Barilla
All other text, and editorial
  coordination: Dalcò Edizioni
Creative photography direction:
  CDA, Carlo De Amici,
  Silvia Ferrario
Photography: About 64,
  Gianmarco Folcolini
Photography assistant:
  Roberta Montalto
Photoshoot production: Nobile
  Agency, Marco Cordera,
  Maya Anderson
Props styling: Silvia Panceri,
  Zuzana Csutortokiova
Food styling: Francesca
  Alberoni, Antonella Pavanello,
  Erica Picco
Transportation: Ermeti srl,
  Marco Ermeti

Printed in China

The publisher would like
to thank Evelyn Battaglia,
Vanessa Bird, João Mota,
Ellie Smith, and Tracey Smith
for their contributions to
the book.